GRITGIRL

Power to Survive Inspired by Grace

SUNDAY BURQUEST

True Potential
REACH THE WORLD

GRIT GIRL
Power to Survive Inspired by Grace

Cover and Interior Page design by True Potential, Inc.

ISBN: 978-1-943852-89-5 (paperback)
ISBN: 978-1-943852-90-1 (ebook)

Library of Congress Control Number: 2018939490

True Potential, Inc.
PO Box 904, Travelers Rest, SC 29690
www.truepotentialmedia.com

Produced and Printed in the United States of America.

CONTENTS

CONTENTS

INTRODUCTION

Sitting alone in a hotel room a single word hit me: GRIT.

My husband came home from work one day with a gift from a woman I didn't personally know. It was a mystery box of sorts with five specific gifts carefully chosen and wrapped in hand-painted tissue paper. One of the items was a gift certificate to a hermitage, a solitude retreat center, something I'd never heard of. The other gifts included a book about prayer, CDs with specific songs individually recorded, and three items of which several made mention of Japanese pearls and the process of how they are formed. Being completely unfamiliar with pearls, I looked up enough information to learn that over a period of time, grit—housed in an oyster at the bottom of the ocean—can be transformed into a pearl. I now know the Holy Spirit had spoken to this woman months earlier about giving me the box and each specific gift inside. Opening the box was exciting—how often does one receive a 'mystery box' from someone they don't know? I opened each gift slowly, one being a blue velvet jewelry box with a necklace. The silver chain had a small pearl with a note attached: NO GRIT NO PEARL. That's when it hit me; I was quiet enough to hear the voice of the Holy Spirit. He gave me the direction I was longing for. *I got the chills.*

> I now know the Holy Spirit had spoken to this woman months earlier about giving me the box and each specific gift inside. Opening the box was exciting— how often does one receive a 'mystery box' from someone they don't know?

Labeled as a 'chatty Kathy' in elementary school and a 'social butterfly' in high school, I was the last one to be alone, *on purpose.* Yet there I was, by myself in Isanti, Minnesota, with a desk, rocking chair, altar, bed, and a loaf of bread. There was no Internet, no Facebook, no Twitter, no cell phone; it was just me and the Holy Spirit. I waited. I listened. I prayed. I had to stop moving, talking, and busying myself with life to get an answer from the only one who could give it to me. Needing direction for my life and ministry, I was desperate to know God's plan for me, knowing that when I do the planning without consulting Him, it's never a good thing.

Having been given the opportunity to be alone and totally free of all distractions, I was able to listen to the Holy Spirit; the idea/concept of being a Grit Girl exploded inside me. I believe we are all girls at heart, stronger than we give ourselves credit for and willing to fight for what we want—*if we know how*. The 'how' is grit. The Merriam Dictionary defines grit as *strength of mind and spirt and an unyielding courage in the face of hardship* (https://www.merriam-webster.com/dictionary/grit). I realized that in my darkest times it was grit that kept me from completely giving up. One of my favorite quotes is by Ann Flounder: "She was strong, and brave, and broken all at once." I love this because I believe it represents all of us. Every woman I know faces situations in which she feels strong, other times she's weak, and yet other times she is brave and afraid at the same time—all while being broken inside. Summed up in four words: NO GRIT NO PEARL.

> The Merriam Dictionary defines grit as *strength of mind and spirt and an unyielding courage in the face of hardship.*

"And so we are transfigured (transformed) like the Messiah, our lives gradually becoming brighter and more beautiful as God enters our lives and we become like him."

2 Corinthians 3:18 (The Message Translation)

CHAPTER 1

GRIT GIRL

WHY GIRT GIRL? ALTHOUGH IT WAS SOMETHING I ALREADY POSSESSED, I couldn't verbalize what 'it' was, until now. I recently walked away from 26 years in ministry with an idea but no plan, *completely depending on Jesus.* I'll be honest and say I floundered for at least a year, trying to find my place, a solid plan to follow, and something to set up my future. I had spent most of my adult life working for one ministry and really didn't know how to be on my own. I was so accustomed to scheduling meetings, training volunteers, preaching and counseling that I felt a little lost without the security blanket of a plan. It wasn't until I spent a weekend in silence that I was quiet enough to hear the voice of the Holy Spirit divulge a plan—Grit Girl.

You may already be thinking, "I don't have grit; I'm full of anxiety and fear. I'm not brave or strong; I am weak." Nothing could be further from the truth! Many of us have believed a lie for so long that it's become our truth. It could be a lie stemming from when you were a little girl—told you were weak or not strong enough to play with the boys. Or maybe in high school a boyfriend or a parent said you were emotionally weak, saying things like, "She can't handle that, so just take care of it for her." Maybe you believed a bigger lie like you were weak because God created women weak—*again not true*. The truth is you are weak on your own; we all are—men and women. However, you are not on your own.

I have chosen to put my trust in Jesus and it's His strength *in me* that makes me strong. My first of three steps to becoming a Grit Girl was to put my **trust** in Jesus. When I did, I realized my strength ultimately comes from Him and *He equips me with grit*.

Step two was having to know He would not just **provide** me with strength, but also I had to **believe** it for myself. I had to believe that strength was already in me. It's easy to believe that someone else is strong, but it's another to believe *you* are strong. For years people have commented on how strong I've been in the midst of difficult situations. I am the first one to admit that my strength is not of my own doing—it's because of Jesus in me. I also try to communicate the times they don't see my weak moments not posted on Instagram. Those times when I'm crying in bed at night or wondering why God let something happen to me. We must remember that when we see others, they're usually at their best; it's rare to find people who are transparent about their weaknesses. When we notice the strength of the women around us, it can be hard not to compare ourselves. We have to remember we are all in different stages of the transformation process. Believing in the power of your God-given strength will provide you with confidence to act on your girt. Even if you don't know it yet, you have the strength to handle anything.

Step three was choosing to believe in the **power** of His strength in me. When I chose to believe I had grit, *I acted like it*. This will manifest differently for each woman and each unique battle she faces. Acting on your grit could mean standing up for yourself, saying no to things that distract from your life. It could mean following a dream you've put on the back burner. Living your life with grit might disappoint others when, suddenly, you choose to have boundaries or say no to others' expectations. Grit allows you to stand up, add to, subtract from, and make the decisions necessary for you to overcome. I've had situations in which I had to be okay with taking extra time to rest, even if it meant attending church online, saying no to fulfilling others' needs, or even letting go of an unhealthy relationship. Taking action is hardly ever easy—it takes guts; it takes grit.

Coming to the realization you are stronger than you thought is a process, and it doesn't happen overnight. Grit without God can be damaging, causing you to make moves that don't benefit you, are hurtful to others, and are simply action for the sake of action. When I'm not clear about my motives or I question if I'm making the right decision, I try praying and asking the Holy Spirit to guide me. Once I put my trust in Jesus and realize I can't survive my challenges alone, I grow confident enough to act on my grit. When a woman truly understands where her strength comes from, she is empowered because she is no longer depending on herself. For most women having confidence in their strength is difficult because their own negative thoughts tell them they are weak and remind them of their flaws. Having grit requires shifting focus from negative thoughts to positive ones. Concentrating on His strength in you is the empowerment you need to act on your grit. *You can do it; you are a grit girl.*

When I think about the difficult times I've experienced—deaths in the family, life-threatening medical issues, and professional challenges—it feels overwhelming. Looking back, I try to focus on the positive God-hugs I received along the way and the grace that helped me make it through. I've had more good experiences than bad; however, it was the setbacks and failures that forced me to look to Jesus and find my grit. Ladies, there is nothing special or out of the ordinary about me, nothing that makes me stronger than the next. My strength is truly not my own. I've simply chosen to put my trust in Jesus rather depending on myself.

I wrote an acronym I use for the word G.R.I.T to help me shape the definition of what it means to be a Grit Girl: Grace, Resilience, Inspiring and Tough.

G GRACE

R RESILIENCE

I INSPIRING

T TOUGH

A Grit Girl is DEPENDENT on GRACE. Do a simple Google search of the word grace, and you'll find variations of the same definition. My favorite reads: "Grace is God's ability in me that allows me to do what I cannot do myself." A Grit Girl understands she is completely dependent on God's grace to face her toughest challenges.

When you depend on His grace, you are a Grit Girl.

A Grit Girl is DEFINED by RESILIENCE. Resilience is the ability to quickly recover from hardship. In the middle of a storm, nothing feels quick; however, when you refuse to be defined by your circumstances, you'll gain confidence in His strength and will realize you can survive anything faster than you'd imagined.

When you are defined by Resilience, you are a Grit Girl.

A Grit Girl is DESTINED to be INSPIRING. Difficult circumstances provide a story, and you are destined to inspire others with that story. The grit you have been equipped with when you choose to put your trust in Jesus is not only for you to survive, but it also gives you the confidence to inspire other women.

When you are destined to inspire, you are a Grit Girl.

A Grit Girl is DESIGNED to be TOUGH. You've been created strong, already possessing the ability to keep pushing forward when it feels like the world is against you. You were designed to by physically, emotionally, and spiritually tough, equipped with everything necessary to handle any situation. A grit girl knows that with NO GRIT, there is NO PEARL.

When you are designed tough, you are a Grit Girl.

CHAPTER 2

GRIT, GRACE & PARENTS

"DAD, CAN WE GO ON A BIKE RIDE?" I WAS STUNNED WHEN HE RESPONDED, "I don't know. Your mom told me I might have to leave." I was only eight years old and remember exactly where I was standing in the living room of our small north Minneapolis home. My dad was an alcoholic, and I knew something was wrong, even at a young age. I clearly remember a handful of situations that made me aware my dad had a problem. The good news is he never treated us in a way that would cause the type of trauma normally associated with having an alcoholic parent. There was never any physical or verbal abuse.

My dad's personality was easy going, a typical second-born personality type. He wasn't tall, and he wasn't large, about 5'7", with a medium build. He was just right. I was born in 1971 to parents who were borderline hippies. My dad's hair was grown out some, and he even had a '70s feathered hairstyle. He was very good looking and his entire life looked incredibly young. He liked kids and kids liked him. All my friends wanted a dad like mine, the kind of dad that actually played with you, took you to fun places, and best of all gave you lots of candy. He would pile our friends and us in our old mustard-yellow rusty station wagon, way before seatbelts were required. He took us to the beach, McDonalds for 25-cent ice cream cones, drive-in movies, and even haunted houses. It didn't seem to matter how many kids he had in tow, but my dad had fun and was patient with every single one of them. I don't know any other man who could take five kids fishing—poles, bait and all—and not lose it. He was always doing something with us like roller-skating—yes, pre-rollerblades—five-mile walks through creek beds, and long bike rides on the beautiful bike paths Minneapolis is known for.

Don't tell my siblings, but Dad liked me best, though we probably all think that. I was the oldest and knew I was special. He would often sing "You are My Sunshine" to me. He did things just for me, like putting a chocolate lamb in my Easter basket every single year instead of a regular chocolate bunny—a feat that involved looking in multiple stores until he found one. One of my favorite memories is the winter, after a large snowfall, that my dad shoveled all the snow in the back yard into one huge pile. He then hooked up the water hose inside the house and sprayed the entire snow pile. We then dug out the inside, making an igloo in our back yard. He even made little shelves on the inside, so I could play kitchen. Whose dad takes the time to build an igloo outside in the cold and then actually plays inside it? Mine!

> Dad and I went camping almost every weekend, just the two of us and, sometimes, our big black German Sheppard named Spanky, in a tiny pup tent. We spent hours playing the card game War and making s'mores by the fire.

Dad and I went camping almost every weekend, just the two of us and, sometimes, our big black German Sheppard named Spanky, in a tiny pup tent. We spent hours playing the card game War and making s'mores by the fire. I remember driving home one weekend and being too tired to stay awake on the back of his motorcycle. We stopped in a small town at the local bar, the kind on the corner where you knew the owners lived in an apartment upstairs, and he knocked on the door. Bars closed on Sundays back then, so he wasn't even sure if anyone would answer. But after just a few knocks on the big wooden doors, a sweet older woman opened them and let us in. My dad explained that I needed some sugar and caffeine to stay awake on the back of the bike for the two-hour ride home. She seemed more than happy to serve up a Coke and a Hershey's candy bar to perk me up, and within 15 minutes we were back on the road. Just in case the sugar fix wore off, my dad literally strapped me to the back of the motorcycle with some sort of belt or rope. I made it home alive.

My mom grew up Catholic, even sending me to Catholic school for Kindergarten and first grade. After she started having children, she began searching for something in her life, not entirely knowing what that 'something' was. She knew she didn't want us to experience growing up in a chaotic atmosphere like she had, so that meant raising us in a Christian home. At the time, she had no idea what that even looked like or what it meant. But when a person starts to search out Jesus, He has a way of making sure He's found. My aunt Barb invited my mom to a neighborhood Bible study during the early years of her marriage. On her first visit, she showed up in her denim cut-off short shorts, hardly knowing anything about the Bible, and was surprised to find that the ladies in the group accepted her 100%, smoking her cigarettes and all. These ladies surrounded her with support and prayed for her alcoholic husband and three children. It was the middle of my kindergarten year when my mom made the decision that changed her life and eventually mine. She invited Jesus into her heart. Even though she didn't know how to be a Christian, especially a Christian wife and mom, she did what she knew—start attending church and reading her Bible. My earliest memories of my mom are waking up every single morning to see her reading her Bible and praying in our little kitchen. My dad never went to church with us, but he never said anything negative about it; he just wasn't interested. As she grew closer to the Lord, my dad's drinking seemed to get worse.

The moment my mom gave her life to Christ—the moment she decided to trust Him—was the exact moment He started to put a plan in place to reach my dad. On a fall weekend trip to his hunting cabin, something special happened. One night after making our dinner with a metal sandwich maker over the fire, we talked for what seemed like hours. I don't completely remember the entire conversation, but I do remember asking my dad a simple question, "Dad, when are you going to ask Jesus into your heart?" I had been going to Sunday school regularly with my mom, soaking in everything I was learning about the Bible and Jesus. I especially loved going to church to see my classroom teachers, Rick and Kim Peterson. I don't remember much about them other than I loved going to Sunday school to see them. I did find Kim on Facebook a couple years ago, and it made my day.

I had my own personal experience with Jesus at my first summer camp through that little church. At the age of six, I remember attending the Brookdale Covent Church summer camp and having an experience in the chapel where I gave my heart to Jesus. I probably didn't have a full understanding of what that meant at the time, but I did know I felt better with Jesus than I did without Him. This is a powerful example of child-like faith, even at such a young age, I knew Jesus was important to me. I knew I wanted to know Him and, in turn, I wanted others to know Him too. I don't think I planned to talk to my dad about Jesus. I certainly wasn't nervous; it was just natural to me.

His answer was sincere, "As soon as somebody tells me how." I was so excited to say, "I can; I can tell you how, Dad!" I had him repeat a simple prayer after me, asking Jesus to forgive his sins and inviting Him into his heart. Even putting myself back in that moment, it makes me feel so thankful that I had easily believed and shared Jesus. My life could have taken a completely different path had it not been for this one simple prayer. One act of grace, one man believing Jesus would accept him, alcoholic and all, because his seven-year-old daughter said so. This moment was what I call a *God-hug*—those times when I knew God did something special for me. He knew I was worried about my dad and his relationship with Jesus, so I believe He set us up *perfectly*. I'm not sure why, but neither of us mentioned it to my mom. You would think I'd be bounding through the door, excited to tell her the news. But, for whatever reason, I didn't tell her, and neither did he. I'm sure he thought if he told her, he would then be accountable to the new relationship He just formed. He just wasn't ready—*yet*.

A few months later, my mom tells a story that I do not remember. One night, our church had a children's program, and I was asked to share a testimony. I must have told my Sunday school teachers, Rick and Kim, about praying with my dad, and they knew it would be a powerful story to share in front of all the parents. I proudly took my spot on the small stage and shared the entire story about my weekend with my dad, our brown-bean sandwiches over the fire, and our prayer. When my mom tells me the story, she points out there was not a dry eye in the audience. My story sent a message to everyone in attendance that day: God will use anyone, even a child, to reach out to someone who needs Him and may not even know it. My dad was at the program that night and con-firmed to my mom that, indeed, He'd asked Jesus into his life. The church leaders also loved the story, asking me to write down the event in my own words, in my own penmanship, and printing it in the church bulletin the next week for the entire church to read. I loved my church; my mom brought my brothers and me every Wednesday night to AWANA, a Bible club for kids similar to the Girl or Boy Scouts. I had a workbook and verses to memorize. I still have my AWANA shirt with all my earned medals and pins. I was the girl in class who was determined to beat everyone else, memorizing the most verses and winning the most challenges. Even at that age, I had a certain level of grit in me. I *had* to be the best, and I was.

That prayer, however, didn't yield an immediate change; transforma-tion takes time. Even though there was an instant inward change in my dad, the process of seeing the results of that change took time. As a child, your concept of time is blurry. While I know Jesus was talking

> My story sent a message to everyone in attendance that day: God will use anyone, even a child, to reach out to someone who needs Him and may not even know it. My dad was at the program that night and confirmed to my mom that, indeed, He'd asked Jesus into his life.

to my dad, internally there had to be a war taking place for his heart and soul. Jesus had forgiven him, yet he couldn't make himself stop the destructive behavior. There are certain situations that I remember, and mostly it's because I am reminded of how they made me feel; *I felt afraid.* I always knew when he came home in the middle of the night drunk because my mom would lock him out, and he'd ring the doorbell again and again until she let him in the house. The noise would always wake me up and I'd be scared, even though I knew it was he outside the house. One time, I came into the living room to find him lying on the couch, eyes black and blue, almost swollen shut with cuts and scrapes all over his face. I don't know how badly the rest of his body was, but I think he was trying to hide it under the hand-knit green and blue afghan my mom had made. He'd driven up an exit ramp on his motorcycle and got into accident. After being taken to the hospital and refusing treatment, he went back out drinking. Although I didn't know about the accident at the time, seeing him banged up scared me.

It became clear that keeping an alcoholic father in the home was detrimental and unsafe. The ice-fishing incident was followed by an accident that caused my mom to finally give him the ultimatum she'd been contemplating for months, one of the hardest things she'd ever done.

My house where I grew up was small, and I mean so small that anytime someone was on the telephone, we all knew it. One weekend in January, my dad took my four-year-old brother, Max, ice fishing at the family cabin. My mom called him to say goodnight, and he excitedly told her how he had fallen through the ice near the shore. Thankfully, he was safe, but mom was furious, especially after Max confirmed my dad had been drinking. That accident haunted her. It became clear that keeping an alcoholic father in the home was detrimental and unsafe. The ice-fishing incident was followed by an accident that caused my mom to finally give him the ultimatum she'd been contemplating for months, one of the hardest things she'd ever done. Having three kids depending on her, no college education, with barely a driver's license, she was scared. But she knew from her own childhood experience that she could not raise us in a home with an alcoholic parent.

That terrifying accident that followed was my dad forcing my mom to let him drive home from a New Year's Eve party. He'd been drinking heavily and insisted on driving home, even though he was in no shape to do so. The party was in a town unfamiliar to my mom, and it was dark and snowing, so she was afraid of having no idea how to get home. All she could think about was getting home safely to us kids where a babysitter was waiting. In her mind she kept repeating, "I just have to get home to my kids." She even asked several people to give her a ride home to her kids. And even though they knew how drunk my dad was, they all refused. Instead of taking her home, he drove her to the local gravel pits and repeatedly threatened to make her get out of the car, in the middle of the night, in the dark, in the snow, in the middle of nowhere. The fear, the desperation, and the anger she must have felt are unimaginable to me. Those are memories that don't disappear, even though he didn't remember any of it the next day.

The situation had reached the tipping point. My mom could feel her anger taking over. For many people, anger is an outward expression of an inward fear. She was afraid we'd grow up like she did, afraid the lights or even the heat could be turned off because of how much of dad's income was wasted on his drinking. Because of my mom's childhood experiences, she barely graduated high school. So now she didn't feel qualified to go into the workforce, and even if she did, what would she do with us kids? She had no support system other than one sister and her husband. Her fear turned into an expression of anger—angry over things that in a 'normal' situation wouldn't cause such rage. She was blamed for my dad's drinking, even being told his drinking was due to her anger issues. The truth was she was experiencing an anger she was unable to control because of the fear driving her, all started by dad's drinking in the first place. It was a vicious cycle, and they were both stuck in it. However, the breaking of that cycle was on its way, working in both of their hearts but in completely different ways.

I'd seen mom cry, plead, and get angry about his drinking. She was doing what she could to protect the kids. She even had me attend an Alcoholics Anonymous Saturday mornings special class designed for kids who had a parent with a drinking problem. I remember walking more than a mile, in the winter, up-hill the entire way—just kidding, not really up-hill—and all I could think about the entire way was the hot chocolate I could have when I finally got there. I thought it was especially awesome no one monitored the self-serve station where I'd combine two packets of hot cocoa mix and load up my hot drink with as many marshmallows as I could fit. I couldn't tell you a thing about what we talked about, who lead the group, or anything about any of the other kids; I just remember the long walk in my moon boots on Saturday mornings—and my hot double cocoa loaded with marshmallows.

I don't remember exactly what was happening with my dad between the time I prayed with him and the day mom gave him the ultimatum—other than the few incidents I remember and the ones mom's told me. However, I do distinctly remember the moment he told me he may be leaving. My heart sank. My thoughts raced—what about bike rides? What about camping? What about the beach and going to the cabin? I didn't know anyone whose parents were divorced. I think I didn't even know what that word was. I literally could not picture what a world without my dad in the home would look like. I'm not sure if I even thought I woud never see him again if he moved out. I had no frame of reference to picture what this would mean for my family. I just knew I was scared—*again*.

It's difficult for a kid to comprehend adult issues. On the one hand, I loved my dad very much. On the other hand, I felt protective of my mom. Somehow, I understood why she had asked him to leave. After giving him the choice, quit or drink, she gave him the weekend to think about it. Sunday night he'd need to pack up and leave if he chose the drinking. My dad chose us—he chose me and chose to quit drinking. For most people, saying they are going to quit an addiction and actually doing it are two entirely different stories. Not my dad. I'm not sure how he did it, but he quit drinking *cold turkey*, and there was a major positive shift in our family. I believe that prayer and the desire to follow Christ are what gave him the ability to quit drinking. One sentence—one decision—changed our family permanently.

While a huge prayer had been answered and my dad was no longer drinking, the coming months were difficult. He never relapsed like so many people do—alcoholism is a disease without cure, only abstinence—but the emotional effect of the drinking didn't change overnight. Like people who make the life-changing decision to allow Jesus into their heart and make Him Lord of their lives, his a journey was one of transformation. The anger, fear, and hurt my mom had felt during the past 10 years did not disappear. The guilt, shame, and anger my dad felt toward my mom wasn't magically erased either. There was an incredible amount of hurt, forgiveness, and grace that they would both need to work through. The coming months, and even years, were hard work, but neither of them quit.

> A few months after the drinking stopped, and the seed from our prayer began to grow, my dad decided to start attending church with us.

A few months after the drinking stopped, and the seed from our prayer began to grow, my dad decided to start attending church with us. My mom had been visiting a newly formed church that was meeting in the auditorium of the local community college. The first time my dad attended, he loved it. He was impressed with the upbeat music, especially the drums, something he'd never seen in church before. He felt that the pastor was speaking right to him through his message, and together my parents decided this was the church for us all. Our lives changed forever on the day my dad chose his family over alcohol, and the entire direction of our family shifted from the brink of disaster to growing together.

Like most kids, I've taken on personality and character traits from both my mom and my dad. I had such a great relationship with my dad that I have never struggled with needing a man's approval. I was always sure he loved me, and that gave me a sense of security and self-assurance. This is a big factor behind why I trust God as my Father. According to the Bible, our dad on earth becomes a picture and example of who God the Father is to us in heaven. If you had a difficult relationship with your dad or felt you couldn't trust him, it can be difficult to trust God. Whereas, in my case, my relationship with my dad gave me a foundation that made it less difficult to trust God. As I look back on the many things that have happened in my life, I can see the qualities of my dad affecting how I react to things, even how I move forward. First, I can trust God because I trusted my dad. Second, I value people—I at least I try too—like my dad valued people. Third, I try to find the positive in even negative situations; my dad was a great example of this.

From my mom, I learned strength and reliance. I also learned to trust God not only because of my dad, but because I watched my mom learn to trust and depend on Him too. For as long as I can remember, when I was a little girl, I'd wake up every morning to see my mom reading her Bible and to hear her pray. In so many ways, this is my mom's story; she has more grit than anyone I know. Part of the reason she put her full dependency on God was because she felt she had no other option; her trust was almost out of desperation. She made the toughest decision of her life when giving my dad that ultimatum and risking him walking out the door completely. Although this was a painful time for her, she was confident God had a plan. My mom was a true example of grit, even way before I knew what that was.

> From my mom, I learned strength and reliance. I also learned to trust God not only because of my dad, but because I watched my mom learn to trust and depend on Him too.

If I had to summarize my childhood, my mom and my dad, it would be with two words: grace and grit. Grace is often described as God's unearned favor and the ability to do through Him what we cannot do for ourselves. My mom had to depend on God's grace to help her survive her childhood experience with an alcoholic father and the early years of my dad's alcoholism. She needed grace to walk in forgiveness toward my dad, to experience healing in her heart, which only Jesus can provide, and the grace to let go of her anger. My dad had to depend on God's grace to live day-to-day without alcohol, to forgive himself, to let go of guilt, and to be the Godly husband and father he was called to be. Both had true grit in their own way—the ability to grow in order to survive. Yes, looking back, I can summarize my childhood in two words—*grace and grit*—*and both came from Jesus.*

A Grit Girl is <u>DEPENDENT</u> on <u>GRACE</u>.

My dad was an example of grace in action. Seeing the transformation from alcoholic to a man living for Christ was a living example that anyone's life can change by simply trusting in Jesus. At the same time my mom demonstrated a level of girt I will never forget. By putting her trust in Jesus, she had the courage to make the toughest decision she'd ever make. Both parents walked dependent on Jesus, and both relied on grace. When you choose Jesus, you choose grace. *When you depend on grace, you are a Grit Girl.*

"He has said to me, 'My grace is sufficient for you [My lovingkindness and My mercy are more than enough—always available—regardless of the situation]; for [My] power is being perfected [and is completed and shows itself most effectively] in [your] weakness. Therefore, I will all the more gladly boast in my weaknesses, so that the power of Christ [may completely enfold me and] may dwell in me.'"

2 Corinthians 12:9 The Amplified Translation

CHAPTER 3

JUGGLING THE ROLES OF WIFE, MOM & PASTOR

WE HAVE A RUNNING JOKE ABOUT MY FAMILY AS COMPARED TO MY HUS-
band's. His is often described as a "Leave it to Beaver" type of family.
Mine—well, quite the opposite—more like "Malcom in the Middle." I think I grew up not much differently than a lot of families.
We had chaos and yelling, but we also knew our parents loved us. To
this day, my siblings and I lock arms when trouble hits, always there
for one another. We are our own brand of grit.

I have classic first-born child personality traits, wanting to please
my parents, getting good grades. The parent-pleasing lasted until I
transferred from a public school to a small Christian school in my
eighth-grade school year. It's a bit ironic, but my rebellious years
started with the influence of the 'Christian' kids at school. It plainly
proves the point that not all families are perfect, especially that not
all 'good' kids are going to make good choices, *even if they are raised*

in Christian homes. I'm sure the bad influence wasn't just the kids and the school. Part of the problem had to do with my age and with the chaos at home.

My eighth-grade year in private school was honestly awful. Most of the students had grown up together, and I was an outsider. My church, where grew up, had taken ownership of the school that year, and many of us church kids found our parents doing everything possible to put us into a Christian environment. Those of us who were new to the school weren't like the rest of the students. Their parents had money, a lot more than our parents who were barely scraping by to afford the tuition. I remember, for the first time in my life, feeling I wasn't enough—more importantly, I felt I didn't *have* enough. One day, this became glaringly obvious when we were changing after gym class in the locker room. I noticed that most of the girls' socks were the brand name Ralph Lauren. I hardly knew what Polo was, let alone that it made expensive socks. I had to babysit for hours to make enough money to buy my own designer jeans, let alone have parents who could buy me insanely expensive socks. It was immediately clear that I didn't measure up to the rest of the girls, *at least in my mind.* It also didn't help that the pastor's son and I shared a pre-teen crush, at least during the first few weeks of the new school year. Once the other girls found out about it, I was a permanent outcast. I spent the entire year trying to fit in, getting the right clothes, and making the right friends. But every single day of that agonizing school year, I felt on the outs. The feeling of not being good enough followed me for years. My mom had no idea how I felt until the next summer when we started talking about my ninth-grade year. Somehow, I was able to convince my parents to let me attend the local public high school where we had moved. I started

> I noticed that most of the girls' socks were the brand name Ralph Lauren. I hardly knew what Polo was, let alone that it made expensive socks. I had to babysit for hours to make enough money to buy my own designer jeans, let alone have parents who could buy me insanely expensive socks.

my last year of middle school at Osseo Senior High. I was scared to death of my first day.

My new school was huge, with more than 500 students. And with my self-confidence severely damaged from the previous private school, I was so nervous that I thought I was going to puke. Anticipating the lunch period was the worst: Who would I sit with? Where would I sit? Where is the cafeteria anyway? Somehow, I don't even remember how I made it through my first day. I did find a friend in one of my first few classes, so I didn't have to eat alone. Over the coming weeks, I made quite a few friends, probably too many. My friends weren't terrible, but they weren't great either—most were not Christian. Even though I was regularly attending my youth group at church and involved with numerous activities, I constantly struggled with wanting to fit in at my new school—wanting, at all costs, to never feel like I had at the Christian school. Like most teenagers, I let my friends become my everything, including the ones to shape my choices. It was in that ninth-grade year that I started to compromise my faith and the values my parents had instilled in me. I couldn't help it, though. I just wanted so badly to be accepted.

My brothers were only a few grade levels behind me; when I was 15, they were 11, 10 and 7. They were smart and learned early that they could blackmail me. I often had to rely on them to help cover my rebellious behavior in a home with strict Christian values. One of our house rules was we were not allowed to listen to non-Christian music. You can imagine that as a teen growing up in the '80s, the absolute best time for music ever, it was difficult to resist the likes of Prince, Madonna, and Def Leppard.

My bedroom was downstairs next to my brothers' room, and for whatever reason, mine was not a completely finished room. The drywall on my ceiling covered only about ¾ of the room, leaving an opening between the drywall and the ceiling joist above. This opening became my favorite 'hiding' spot for things I shouldn't have had—one thing being my music cassettes. Our bedrooms shared a closet. In fact, if you lifted a ceiling tile from their side, you could get from their room to the back side of my closet. This came in handy particularly one afternoon. I had my radio set to KDWB 101.3, the local top-hit station; the one I was strictly prohibited by my parents from listening. I had left my radio quietly on my favorite radio station while I showered in the bathroom next door, thinking I'd be quick. When I tried to return to my room, I discovered that I had somehow left the lock in place, my door had shut, and I was locked out of my room. In any normal circumstance, a kid would yell for a parent to come figure out how to get the door opened. Not me. I panicked because my radio was on, and it wasn't set to Christian music. I was going to be in huge trouble. I had no choice but to get my brothers involved. Together, we came up with a plan. Tying a rope around the legs of my youngest brother, Timmy, we lifted him up to the ceiling of the boy's closet, moved a ceiling tile, and lowered him into my side of the closet in my room. He opened the door and my parents were none the wiser. My joy at out-witting my parents was short lived because my brothers made sure I knew I now owed them. Somehow, they figured out where my 'ceiling stash' was, and they would 'borrow' my stuff. "Let us listen to your Def Leppard tape, or we'll tell mom," they threatened. Moving forward, we agreed never to tell on one another—*ever*.

I had major ups and downs in my relationship with Jesus during my teenage years. It was difficult for me to follow Him while trying to fit in with my friends at the same time. I was often conflicted. I was also often grounded. In fact, I spent most of my summers grounded from friends and phone. But the one thing I was not grounded from was church or church camp. Summer camp was always my favorite week of summer. My parents had to work hard to save up enough money to send us, and we went every year. And every year, I would again dedicate my life to Jesus, determined to stick close to Him and His ways. I stayed involved in youth group, making video announcements and serving on leadership teams—all the while making poor choices with my non-Christian friends. Even though those years were difficult, I knew in my heart that Jesus would never give up on me and that His grace was always extended to me. His grace kept calling me back, no matter how many times I messed up. Only because of His love did I keep coming back to Him.

After graduating from high school, I was lost. I considered going to college to be a fitness instructor as a safe choice because I didn't know what else to do. Ever since I can remember, I had a desire to serve God. I simply had no idea what that looked like for my life moving forward. My mentor, Susan Fletcher, reminded me one day that I had always talked about following Jesus and serving Him, so she suggested Bible college. The minute she said it, I knew she was right. When you know something is right, it's right. That was the moment that I decided whole-heartedly I'd be serving Jesus the rest of my life, wanting and willing to train for and eventually serve in full-time ministry. Within a two-week time period, I had registered and been accepted to a Bible college in Tulsa, Oklahoma, and moved down there. It all happened so fast that I hardly remember packing. But I do remember standing in the parking lot of my apartment building alone, with tears rolling down my cheeks as my parents drove away after moving me in.

> I had major ups and downs in my relationship with Jesus during my teenage years. It was difficult for me to follow Him while trying to fit in with my friends at the same time. I was often conflicted.

I was eighteen, in a new state, with no friends, and starting a new college in two days. Again, panic. Like something I just could not escape, those same questions from my eighth-grade year were back again—Will I fit in? How will I find friends? What if I feel like an outcast? I'm sure such feelings and thoughts are typical for most students, whether starting high school or college. I woke up the first day of classes and decided I *had* to ignore these negative thoughts. Just short of saying it out loud, I thought *Put on your big girl panties, smile, and go make friends; you can do this*. Grit was pushing me through my insecurities. Somehow, on that first day, I made several friends, but three became my best buddies. To this day, 25 years later, we're still best friends—*God-hug*.

Bible college was fun but uneventful. I finished my two-year program with an emphasis on mission work. I love to travel, and I love to serve people in other nations, especially Africa. Ironically, when I was a teenager, I would think to myself *I don't want to serve God because if I do, He'll make me live in Africa*. I now had no idea what things I thought would be bad about living in Africa—probably not seeing my family. But more ironically, I've been there six times now and even lived in Kenya for a month. I think God has a real sense of humor about these things. After graduation, I moved back home and was offered a position as receptionist at the church where I'd grown up.

That same year, a 26-year-old whose family had started attending the church while I was away at Bible college, was hired in the same ministry as a new 4th grade teacher—Jeff Burquest, the kids called him Mr. B, and he was an instant hit with the school. After being away for a little more than two years, I needed to re-connect and meet people, especially as a 19-year-old who had outgrown youth group. Jeff's family was new to the church, so he and I found ourselves going to the young adult group to meet friends. The group was great, and we all hung out a lot, doing fun activities while having Bible studies and getting involved at church.

> I had my ministry degree from Bible college, but I wasn't exactly sure where God was taking me quite yet, so I did volunteer work by teaching the 3-year-olds Bible class on Sunday mornings.

I had my ministry degree from Bible college, but I wasn't exactly sure where God was taking me quite yet, so I did volunteer work by teaching the 3-year-olds Bible class on Sunday mornings. Jeff also volunteered with kids but in the bus ministry department. Our paths then started to cross often.

Jeff's sister, Joy, who was my age, was also attending the young adult group. We became friends, and I eventually got up the courage to ask her about Jeff. She was surprised but thought it was great I liked him. Later I found out Jeff liked me too. He was just nervous that people would think our age gap of seven years was too wide. Joy and I pulled off a scheme one night, after group let out, to go eat, forcing Jeff to have to give me a ride home. We talked in his car for more than four hours that night. Even though I was starting to feel so sick, I was excited to be having such a great conversation with him. I didn't care how sick I felt. That night, he asked me out on our first date.

Our first date was fun, nothing out of the ordinary. We attended the wedding of one of his best friends. It was the beginning of January, and we were dating and working for the same ministry. Even though we weren't in the same building while we volunteered in the children's ministry area, it felt like things were aligning for us perfectly. On March 26, Jeff asked me to marry him. Of course, I said yes. I always believed that if I put my trust in Jesus, He would lead me to the right man, and I'd know it. I knew that man was Jeff in just a couple of weeks after we started dating, and he felt exactly the same way. With our pastor, we chose July 17, 1992 as our wedding daete, just a little more than two months after Jeff's proposal. The wedding was perfect and everything I could have hoped for—all except my little brother, Timmy, a fourth grader, who was not at all happy about his big sister marrying his teacher. To this day, the photos of him in my wedding are hilarious. The look on his face is priceless; he was so mad.

Jeff and I had the normal disagreements that all newlyweds have as we got accustomed to living with each other, sharing everything and learning how to be a good husband and wife. We shifted our volunteering time at church in order to do it together. We started leading the 4-to-5-year-olds Bible class every Sunday night at church; we did this for almost eight years. It was the first time we served together at church. We had fun coming up with ideas for the class. I had the experience with preschoolers, and he, of course, knew how to handle and lead a classroom. Together we made a great teaching team.

On May 31, 1994 we had our first son, Jeffrey Carter; we called him Carter. I quit my job as the receptionist at church to be home with him, something I'd always wanted to do. Because I was at home, I was able to start attending the women's group at church on Tuesday mornings, something I'd looked forward to since the day we got married. I knew the group would help me grow as a mom and as a wife.

Soon after starting to attend the group, I joined the leadership team—first as an assistant and shortly after as a small group leader. I loved leading my small group of moms, anywhere from 8 to 15 time each week. Eventually, I was asked periodically to teach the combined large group, and I absolutely loved it. I learned so much from my time in the group. I was a leader there for almost 12 years, assisting, teaching and mentoring women, especially moms. I loved speaking into the lives of the women in the group, and I was learning just as much as they were, and we all, so badly, just wanted to do our best. My heart for women grew in this ministry. I encountered so many hurting women and found myself reaching out to them by praying and encouraging them. I was relatable because I was real. To me those are the best kind of people to learn from. The leader of our group was also like that. I probably learned how to be authentic from her. I could share messages about getting closer to God and dealing with poopy diapers and Goldfish crackers at the same time and do it with humor and grace.

Being a stay-at-home mom was amazing, the hardest thing on the planet, but still 100% worth it. Before Carter was a year old, Jeff and I realized that we'd need to bring home more than Jeff's income alone. I was re-hired at church as the pre-school children's ministry assistant. Looking back, I'm still not sure how I taught Bible class on Sunday nights, lead a small group of women on Tuesday mornings, and put in almost 30 hours a week in the children ministry. I had no official title for the various positions I held and no one pointing out that I was doing a lot; there was a grace to do it. I find that no matter what I am doing, if I put my trust in Jesus, He opens the doors to where He wants me to be. When He gives me the opportunity, He also provides the grace needed to do it. In 1996 we had our second son, Jeffrey Brock. In 1998 we gad our third, Jeffrey Tucker.

You may be asking yourself a question just about now: Did she really name all three of her sons Jeffrey as a first name? When Jeff and I decided on the name Carter, the only middle name I wanted to use was my husband's, but I didn't like the sound of Carter Jeffrey, so we went with Jefferey Carter, although he goes by his first name. Once we decided on Brock for our second son, the same was true. You can't have two boys with the same first name, so Tucker also got Jeffrey as a first name too. My husband is so embarrassed about this, but he let me have my way. I love their names, even though I drove the insurance people crazy trying to figure out their paperwork.

Tucker was born in 1998, and I again quit my job at church. I had worked in the children's ministry for nearly six years and was ready to be home with my three little boys. I was still in leadership in the women's group and still teaching Bible class with Jeff on Sunday nights. Throughout those six years, Jeff's position had changed drastically. After several promotions, he became the high school principal, just under the school superintendent. We were a young family, working at our church, volunteering at church, and doing the best we could to raise our boys right. On many days my brain felt like play-doh, but I knew we were right in the middle of God's will for our lives. When the days were exhausting or the kids were driving me nuts, I simply had to depend on God's grace and keep going. Honestly, I believe all moms have grit. Although some may feel overwhelmed by fruit snacks and muddy toes, they don't quit. They keep pushing. *If you are a mom, then you are a grit girl.*

> I was a leader there for almost 12 years, assisting, teaching and mentoring women, especially moms. I loved speaking into the lives of the women in the group, and I was learning just as much as they were, and we all, so badly, just wanted to do our best. My heart for women grew in this ministry.

A Grit Girl is <u>DEPENDENT</u> on <u>GRACE</u>.

Whether you are a mom, wife, professional or all three, as women we tend to be hardest on ourselves. Grace isn't just something you need to extend to others; you need to accept it for yourself, shortcomings and all. You're doing a fabulous job at whatever you are doing. You know you're not perfect and that's okay because you give yourself grace. *You are a Grit Girl.*

"Therefore, let us [with privilege] approach the throne of grace [that is, the throne of God's gracious favor] with confidence and without fear, so that we may receive mercy [for our failures] and find [His amazing] grace to help in time of need [an appropriate blessing, coming just at the right moment]."

Hebrews 4:16 The Amplified Bible

CHAPTER 4

DISCOVERING GRIT I

I WAS PREGNANT WITH MY THIRD SON, CHOPPING VEGGIES FOR DINNER when my mom called. She'd been at the doctor with my dad. I don't even know what precipitated the appointment. The news wasn't good; he was diagnosed with a cancer so rare the medical community at that time only knew of 140 cases in the entire world. I stood in my kitchen, staring at the vegetables. My head was spinning. Did she just say *cancer?* He was only 47 years old. From appearances, he looked healthy and was always very young. People regularly commented on how young both of my parents looked.

My dad was not an alarmist; in fact, he was the complete opposite. Most people would describe him as laid back, You could even say it took a lot to rattle his cage. Whether it was a family emergency, a difficult co-worker, or issues with one of our cars, in every situation it took a lot to get my dad upset. Of my two parents, he was the calm one—total opposites. I'd seen him rightly and wrongly upset, but in either case it took a lot to get him to that point.

Even when we acted up as kids, it took a lot to get him mad. But if we pushed him to the point of being angry, we knew we were in big trouble. One story particularly stands out, even though it wasn't at the time; I now find it rather hilarious. One night at dinner when I was 16 years old, I was arguing with my mom. The argument lasted for some time, with my dad periodically interjecting but not really reacting. I continued to mouth off to my mom, who was pregnant with my sister at the time. I stormed into the bathroom to mess with my hair. I was ready to go out with my friends for the night, hair and make-up done, wearing a black and hot pink sweater from Express (the coolest place to shop at the time) and black jeans. I stomped off in my black boots. I don't even remember the last thing I said to my mom. As I was making final touches to my hair, I heard footsteps coming my way. Before I knew it, my dad grabbed me and pushed be backwards into an already full bath tub, completely dunking me. I jumped up screaming, "He's going to drown me!" My mom ran in, yelling at my dad while I stood there in the bathtub looking like a drowned rat. "Don't ever talk to your mother like that again," he stated without even raising his voice. I stood in the bathroom crying, mostly in shock at how my dad had reacted and because my make-up and hair were totally ruined. He returned to the dinner table where my brothers sat wide eyed, having hardly ever seen my dad get pushed to his limit. He continued from the kitchen table, "Next time, I will drown you. Stop lying and lipping off to your pregnant mom!" My brother Lucas, stared right at my dad and quietly said, "You wouldn't *really* drown her." On paper you may be thinking this sounds awful. But honestly, I had it coming. We all laugh about it now. This story is a perfect example of my dad—sit back, not react, be patient, and then bam! If you pushed too far, you knew it.

It was surprising that when he was told he had cancer, he didn't cry or even show he was upset. I knew he had to be scared, but outwardly

> Before I knew it, my dad grabbed me and pushed be backwards into an already full bath tub, completely dunking me. I jumped up screaming, "He's going to drown me!"

he showed complete faith in the healing power of Jesus. He actually took two weeks off from work just to read His Bible, spend time in prayer, and build up his faith. The doctors scheduled a surgery just a few weeks after his diagnosis, concerned that if the cancer spread, it could result in the possible removal of his bladder. The mass was successfully removed, and his follow up treatment was radiation—thankfully, no chemotherapy. Those few months I was worried about my dad, but his calm demeanor helped put me at ease. Following everything suggested by his doctors, combined with the power of prayer, he was told he was cancer free less than six months after the diagnosis.

I was beyond relieved that the cancer was gone. It was so important to me for my boys to have my dad around; they called him papa. It was no surprise he liked to play with his grandkids. He bought the boys night vision googles, and while babysitting one night, he played hide-and-go-seek in the dark with their new googles; they thought it was so cool. He even took them to his cabin for the weekend when Carter and Brock were 3 and 5. Some dads wouldn't want to take kids that young for the weekend alone, but it was no problem for papa.

Just about the time I felt life was going back to normal, feeling grateful my dad was okay, he was diagnosed with cancer a second time. Something felt different this time, even though my dad once again seemed not to be worried. This time the cancer showed up as a spot on his spine. The doctors recommended a 28-day radiation regime. I don't think my dad told many people about the returned cancer; he was quiet about the things that bothered him, always one to focus on helping others through their difficult situations rather than focus on his own. One thing everyone knew about my dad was that he was a hard worker, working as a foreman at Onan Companies for more than thirty years. His work ethic was strong, going every day for his radiation treatment and going right back to work as if he'd just gone out for a quick errand. After finishing the treatment, he was once again cancer free, and I again breathed a sigh of relief as did the rest of my family.

Cancer struck a third time. It was less than six months after finishing the radiation for his spine. At first, he played it off as if he just had a bad cold. One night when he came over with an oxygen tank and oxygen line in his nose, I just knew in my gut this could not possibly be just a cold. I would lay awake at night wondering how many times one person could dodge the 'cancer' bullet. I tossed and turned many nights thinking about what could possibly be going on with him, worried that beating it three times seemed impossible. I repeatedly asked him if his new doctor was making sure of no underlying issue to the lack of oxygen. I even asked him one day, "Dad, does your new doctor know you had cancer? Does she know she should be paying very close attention to your health?" As usual he brushed the questions aside, pretending everything was fine and changing the subject to the last movie we'd seen together. He had a way of putting those around him at ease because of how laid back he was. Even though he kept assuring me he'd be fine, he started asking me unnerving questions like, "Do you want your grandmother's glass serving pieces?"

I'm not entirely sure if his new medication was affecting him emotionally, but my dad was dealing with depression. I tried talking to him, inviting him over, asking him to spend time with the boys, and I prayed for him continually. I now know those with depression don't have the ability to do what's necessary to pull themselves out. I cannot express how helpless I felt. After spending hours on the phone with him, I couldn't seem to help him. I would get off our phone calls and feel utterly defeated. Here I am mentoring women, teaching kids, serving Jesus to the best of my ability, but I could not help my own dad. I would pray at night, asking Jesus to show my dad how much he was loved, asking for grace for my dad to push through whatever was causing the depression. I had a few ideas of what was happening in his mind and in his heart, but I had no idea how to make it better for him; he was hurting, and as much as I tried, I couldn't fix it.

I received a call one afternoon that he'd been taken by ambulance to the hospital due to shortness of breath. A wave of panic washed over me. In my heart I knew this was not going to be a quick visit to the emergency room. As fast as I could, I packed up my youngest son and dropped him off at my in-laws, knowing Jeff could bring our other two boys home from school. The twenty-minute drive to Mercy Hospital felt like an eternity. I swear I hit every single red light possible trying to get there. When I arrived, my mom was already back in the room with dad. I came in almost out of breath, and he just smiled and cracked some sort of joke, *so typical of him*. We asked him all sorts of questions, but he continually dodged giving us straight answers. I tried to be patient. I mean the man *was* having a hard time breathing, but I desperately wanted to know what was really going on. My dad couldn't or wouldn't tell us what was going on, and the nurse couldn't tell us much more. I just knew in my gut it wasn't good. By the time they were able to admit him to a room in the hospital, it was well after 5pm, and the doctor was gone for the day. We'd have to wait an agonizing night to find out *anything*. I finally went home around 9pm, resigned to the fact I wasn't getting any useful information, and I really couldn't do anything to improve the situation. I went home to Jeff and my three little boys, who were 18 months and 4 and 6 years, to attempt to sleep. Not surprisingly, I tossed and turned all night, but I was at the hospital early the next morning.

The first thing I did, after checking on dad, was ask the nurse for the doctor's phone number and immediately called him. I'd never met any of my dad's doctors and in this case, I was glad because our conversation made the hair on my arms stick straight up. "I'm here with my dad, Gary Farrand, and we don't understand what is happening. I have a brother in Tulsa and I need to know if he needs to be here. How much time does he have?" I asked, shaking while trying to hold the phone up to my ear. His response was quick and cold, "Yesterday." I think I may have hung up on him. I couldn't believe was I was hearing. Even though I knew my dad hadn't been forthcoming with his true medical condition, I was certainly not expecting the answer I received. As upset as I was with the doctor for his cold delivery,

> One night when he came over with an oxygen tank and oxygen line in his nose, I just knew in my gut this could not possibly be just a cold. I would lay awake at night wondering how many times one person could dodge the 'cancer' bullet.

the fact that my dad purposely hid it from us was far worse. I kept thinking, *How could you do this to me?*

The following evening, I came home to try to sleep but in the middle of the night received a call from one of his nurses. She explained his medications were making him hallucinate. He was getting out of bed and wandering the halls in his hospital gown, randomly walking into other patients' rooms. While the thought of this made me chuckle a bit, I knew I needed to be there. I drove back to the hospital around 2 am, and from that night forward, I slept on the cold floor of his hospital room on a pile of blankets. It made me feel close to him again, like we were on one of our camping weekends—except in this case, the roles were reversed. I was the one taking care of him. Basically, my brother Lucas and I were the ones doing everything possible to make him smile with movies and card games. We even ate black jelly beans. I might add: To this day, I have a slight issue with eating more than my fair share every spring.

> I looked him in the eyes while gently squeezing his hand and said, "Dad, you were a really good dad." I knew he heard me because he squeezed back, his eyes locked with mine, and one tear streamed out from the side of one eye.

Over the next week, I spent most of my hours with dad at the hospital. My amazing in-laws, Myron and Judy, babysat my youngest while my other two kids were in school. My brother Max flew in from Tulsa, Oklahoma, and together, Max, Lucas, my mom and I spent most of our time at the hospital. My two youngest siblings, Kelsey and Tim, 12 and 17, came to visit periodically, but it was much harder on them to be there. They were both in school and honestly it was too much for them to handle at their age. It was actually better for them to be preoccupied with school and sports.

Over the next six days, we rented funny movies, along with any type of science fiction movies, because that's what my dad liked. He loved the late John Candy and Steve Martin. My dad loved movies in general and took us to the theater quite often. I'm sure it's the reason I love going to movies so much. We limited dad's visitors due to how tired he was and the seriousness of the situation. Family members came—his sisters and just a couple of co-workers. One afternoon, while dad talked with a visitor, I took a quick nap in the waiting room, trying to close my eyes for a few moments. When I came back, he was alone and sitting half way up with a breathing contraption over his face. I have no idea what it was called, but it made his breathing loud and forced, so he pretended to be an Imperial Storm Trooper from Star Wars. I laughed so hard I cried. I learned something while I was spending time with him: I was told some people perk up to give a false sense of improvement as they near heaven's door. One afternoon, my dad's breathing was a little better. He almost seemed like he was turning a good corner. I was relieved to have a few moments alone with him to share some exciting news. I'll be forever grateful I had the opportunity to make him the first person I told I was pregnant with my fourth baby, only 11 weeks along. Having this chance felt like another God-hug. He told me it was a girl and he was right. He also said she'd have red hair, which I think was just wishful thinking because my little sister, Kelsey, had beautiful red hair. I'm sure my brothers' versions of those days at the hospital differ from mine, but I like to remember us like it used to be when we camped in our little tent in the woods.

By day seven in the hospital, the breathing tubes were removed, except for a low dose of oxygen. The nurse explained he wasn't in pain and that his breathing would continually slow down until it stopped as if he were falling asleep. He seemed almost comatose when I had another moment alone with him, aside from his nurse who made sure I knew he could not only hear me but could also understand me. I sat next to his bed, holding his hand, standing up and getting closer to his face. I looked him in the eyes while gently squeezing his hand and said, "Dad, you were a really good dad." I knew he heard me because he squeezed back, his eyes locked with mine, and one tear streamed out from the side of one eye. A few short hours later, he passed from this life to the next. I wish I could have seen his entrance into heaven—my grandma and nephew Hunter waiting for him. He was finally free of pain. Cancer is a terrible thing, stealing joy and life from families. It took my dad's life at the young age of fifty. My only solace is the Bible promises that I will see him again someday. *I have hope.*

The following days were a whirlwind, planning the funeral and making all sorts of arrangements. I will, however, forever remember the next day when my mom and I were at the crematory. We had to decide if we wanted to purchase a container for his ashes. They had everything from plain urns, to statues, to necklaces. We were so over-tired and emotionally exhausted that we cried and laughed hard at the absurd options. I'm sure everyone around us thought we had completely lost it. I spent hours shopping for a black dress that wouldn't give away my pregnancy. But let's face it, with child number four, you aren't hiding much for long. Church took care of most of the funeral details, other than the elegies. I shared both heartfelt and funny stories. I had the crowd laughing as I explained I was so thrilled my dad had left me his Troll doll collection that he was sure would be worth money someday. The funeral and reception were nice, but I just wanted them to be over, although they did provide a great distraction from thinking about the fact that my dad was gone.

It seemed like only a few days had passed and I was back at home, being mom, alone with my thoughts. Everything happened so quickly that I never took the time to stop and think about what had actually happened. One morning I realized I was mad. Tucker, at one and a half, had a habit of asking for the same thing again and again and again until it was literally in his hand. He'd ask for apple juice and the entire time I was getting out the sippy cup and pour the juice, he would still be continually asking. That particular day, it wasn't just annoying; it made me mad. After looking at his blonde little head and blue eyes, I realized I wasn't even mad about his incessant asking. I was mad at the entire situation I had just experienced during the last two weeks. I was angry at cancer; I was even angry *at my dad.* How dare he not fight harder? He could have fought harder for the 5 kids, 3 grandsons and the 14 grandchildren yet to come. He was as good a papa as he was a dad, playing hide-and-go-seek in the dark, taking the boys fishing, and having squirt gun fights with them. It was maddening to know he would miss out on their lives, and they'd grow up without him.

My dad's passing was going to be especially difficult for my youngest brother, Tim, just months away from graduating high school and my little sister, Kelsey, who was in seventh grade. The past few years had been rough with my dad not only going through cancer but also with the depression he had been battling. He just wasn't the same during those last two years. We gave him a hard time because he called Kelsey 'my little muffin,' making us all roll our eyes every time he said it, and he spent a lot of his time taking Tim to basketball and baseball practices and games. It was a heartbreaking situation. I tried not to think about it because with my own little family at home, there didn't seem too much I could do to help them.

Like most people, I experienced stages of emotion and grief as I dealt with my dad's death. Often, hurt manifests itself as anger in our lives. I was angry because deep down I felt my dad left me, even though I knew he didn't really, but *that's how I felt*. What started as anger towards him—and I dare say even God—eventually turned to compassion. I know that on paper having emotions swing from anger to compassion may seem like a giant leap, but transformation didn't happen overnight; it took time. I remember telling myself to snap out of it, he didn't leave you on purpose, *he was sick*. I began thinking less about myself and more about how my dad must have felt in those last years of his life. Compassion welled up on the inside of me when I thought about all the long phone conversations we'd had, in which I tried my hardest to get him to 'snap out of it.' The reality is there is no 'snapping out of depression.' It has the power to keep people trapped in a state of sadness that usually does not represent who they really are. As I've matured and even experienced depression myself, I now know it isn't something a person can just turn off. If it were that easy, he would have done it. There are still days I feel mad that he's gone and a fleeting thought here and there of feeling mad at him, but it's mostly because I miss him so badly and wish my kids had their papa around.

> I was angry because deep down I felt my dad left me, even though I knew he didn't really, but *that's how I felt*. What started as anger towards him—and I dare say even God—eventually turned to compassion.

I also had to stop and ask myself why I was mad at God, knowing this wasn't His doing. I had to re-evaluate my trust in Him and ask myself some hard questions. Why am I mad at God when He didn't give my dad cancer? The truth is God is good. He doesn't go around giving people cancer. He is the author of life. However, we live in a world where even Jesus promised we'd have trials and tribulations. The good news is that isn't the end of what Jesus promised. He also said, "I will never leave you or forsake you." No matter how difficult the situation we are facing is, He is always there. I also had to remember that feelings are fickle and just because I feel anger, it doesn't mean it's the way I have to live, but it also doesn't mean I'm justified in feeling that way. During those first two months, my feelings changed hour by hour, day by day.

> Why am I mad at God when He didn't give my dad cancer? The truth is God is good. He doesn't go around giving people cancer. He is the author of life. However, we live in a world where even Jesus promised we'd have trials and tribulations. The good news is that isn't the end of what Jesus promised.

Two months after my dad's passing while I was facing the fact he was no longer around, I basically didn't feel like doing anything. I didn't feel like leaving the house if I didn't absolutely have to do so. I didn't even feel like playing with the kids—to be completely transparent, I didn't really enjoy 'playing' on a good day.

Along with my anger, I felt sorry for myself, convinced no one else had experienced such a great loss. Of course, the truth is, a lot of people have been through what I was facing. In fact, many have been through worse. The thing is that I'm not really a 'feel sorry for myself' type of gal, and I'm definitely not a 'stay home and be sad' gal either. Those feelings, therefore, didn't last longer than two months. There it was—grit deep inside of me, a trait that would not allow me to stay in a funk, feeling sad and isolated. It gave me the desire to go back to being me.

I really didn't *do* anything out of the ordinary to move past the grief. In fact, most of what I did had less to do with actions and more to do with *my thoughts*. First, I chose to concentrate on how grateful I was for my dad's life, even the Troll dolls he left me, instead of obsessing about his death. Second, I talked to Jesus about my feelings. Instead of trying to fix it on my own, I poured my heart out to the only person who can truly take away the pain. I had to admit happiness was a choice and isn't based on my circumstances. Simply choosing to be happy was by no means an instant fix. For me it meant actually faking that everything was fine until my feelings followed. I tried to decipher whether I wanted to be the girl whose dad died of cancer or the girl who had an amazing dad. Both are true, of course, but it was my choice to decide where my thoughts and feelings would reside.

Over the years, memories, photos, movies, and even certain candy remind me of him, and I'm tempted to allow anger or sadness to creep into my thoughts again. It takes practice to choose happiness repeatedly. The definition of resilience is *the capacity to recover from difficulty*. It's that fighting spirit that causes people to keep pushing through the darkness they are experiencing. Eventually, life was back to normal. It was as if *I were the grit girl I knew I could be.*

A Grit Girl is <u>DEFINED</u> by <u>RESILIENCE</u>.

Being resilient doesn't mean you ignore failure or loss. It simply means you have the ability to recover from it. You don't have to be stuck in a place where setbacks define you, instead you can choose happiness by putting your trust in Jesus, depending on His grace and choosing to concentrate on positive thoughts.

A Grit Girl isn't defined by her setbacks; she's defined by resilience.

"But we do not want you to be uninformed, brothers, about those who are asleep, that you may not grieve as others do who have no hope."

I Thessalonians 4:13–14 The English Standard Version

CHAPTER 5

DISCOVERING GRIT II

MY DAUGHTER, KENNEDY FARRAND MARIE, WAS BORN ON OCTOBER 10, 2000. I convinced Jeff to give her two middle names, Farrand—my maiden name, in honor of my dad—and Marie, same middle name as mine. I was beyond excited to finally be buying pink hair bows. I literally could have exploded. In fact, I was so thrilled to have a little girl to dress up that Kennedy's hair bow collection got so big that it became the envy of my cousins and friends who had daughters. Shortly after Kennedy was born, I took a new career position coordinating church weddings, and Jeff continued as the high school principal at the church's school. In 2001, the day of the September 11 terrorist attacks in New York, Jeff and I had an appointment with our pastor. We were both offered the position of youth pastors at the church and after praying about it, accepted. Just two weeks later we were officially given the title and the responsibilities of leading a large youth group. We put in many hours and loved it. Raising four kids and serving in full-time ministry was crazy at times, but we knew it was exactly the place God wanted us to be.

Within three years, it became increasingly clear that as our kids were getting bigger. We were going to need more space. After selecting a REALTOR®, we started looking at houses, which was a nightmare. Finding time to see houses was tricky because of Jeff's work schedule and having to take four kids along in the evening. It was no picnic. We looked at four houses in our price range, and all I could see was a long list of updates we'd need to do. On top of the homes feeling dated, not one of them had a fenced in yard. Compared to our one-acre, fenced-in yard, a move wasn't worth us having a bigger house with a smaller yard. We were both frustrated when Jeff eventually suggested adding on to our existing split-level house. The idea of a house with an add-on was not great for me; in my experience, they never look quite right.

Jeff is a practical thinker and assured me we'd be able to add square footage onto our existing home with a promise it would be seamless, and he was right. My father-in-law, Myron, could build anything. In fact, a year earlier, he built a huge, beautiful barn, almost entirely for the grandkids. The upstairs ceilings are more than twenty-feet high, and the main barn room has four different basketball hoops, all at varying heights to make sure each grandchild can reach one. He retired young, so he was often willing to jump in and offer help to any of four kids needing his assistance and expertise. Myron spent many days helping Jeff with the addition. As a direct result of his help, we saved thousands of dollars in labor. He worked hard, but as the weeks went on, he seemed to get tired; *it was so unlike him.*

Being a farmer and an extremely hard worker, Myron wasn't one to visit the doctor unless he was truly sick, which was almost never. When he couldn't shake what he thought was a lingering virus, he finally made a doctor's appointment. The first assessment: he was carrying parasite from the beavers in his pond. He'd been fighting on and off with them all summer as they kept damming the creek running through his land. He often removed the pile of branches the beavers used to block the waterway. The doctor assumed he'd been exposed to a beaver parasite from putting his hands in the water. It sounded farfetched, but I guess it happens. Myron's condition didn't improve after a full cycle of antibiotics. In fact, he was feeling worse and noticeably tired. Even though I felt terrible, he continued to help Jeff with the addition.

He continued to visit the doctor, and they attempted to find an explanation for the illness. After further testing, the doctor delivered the news: Non-Hodgkin's Lymphoma. In the world of cancer, doctors use the words "the best kind of cancer to have" and were hopeful regarding the outcome. Still, Jeff, his mother—Judy, his siblings—Phil, Joy and Robyn, and me were devastated. I had just been through this two years earlier, and all I could think was *Not again. Not Myron.* The thought of walking through this situation again was daunting, and even though I felt sick to my stomach, I tried to be strong for Jeff.

Over the coming months, Myron endured chemotherapy and radiation, experiencing terrible side effects. In December 2001, he was declared cancer free; he'd beat it! We celebrated with a dinner at a nice restaurant not far from our house. Christmas was extra special that year because we believed Myron's cancer and the horrible treatment he endured were behind us. Jeff and Myron bundled the kids up and pulled them behind a snowmobile on a sled, something they loved doing. I have a photo of Myron and Kennedy from that night; she, with bright red cheeks, was bundled up in her snowsuit. It's one of her favorite photos. In the summer months, he would carry her around the farm on his shoulders, telling her the birds were singing her name, "Kennedy-dee-dee-dee." It was so sweet.

As January arrived, things took a downward turn for Myron. He started having terrible headaches. After CT scans and blood work, the diagnosis was even more devastating than the first time. The scans revealed a tumor growing in his brain, and the doctors weren't sure they could stop it. It was difficult to comprehend how this man who oozed godly character, exercised daily, never drank, smoked or did drugs, was being over-taken by the evil of cancer. The coming months were difficult as I watched my in-laws go through what I had just experienced with the passing of my dad. I remember sitting in my jetted bathtub one night for more than an hour, sobbing. "God, I don't understand why this is happening again." Myron was suffering, and it was difficult to watch. He was in so much pain. He prayed; we all prayed, and we all believed he'd have a miracle.

Once again, I needed to remember that Jesus never promised a perfect life. In fact, perfect isn't even a possibility in a fallen world. I had to remember that Jesus didn't change, even if my circumstances had. The feelings of anger I felt when I lost my dad started to come to the surface again. Because the Bible describes God as a Father, I thought about how I felt when my kids were mad at me. I'd heard the occasional, "I'm mad at you" or 'I don't like you anymore" from my own kids. In fact, when Tucker was little, he used to say, "I have really angry eyebrows at you Mom." I didn't punish him, yell at him, or even take it personally when he—or any of my kids—got angry with me. I was happy they could express their feelings, but at the same time I tried my best not to laugh at them. Sometimes, I try to imagine what Father God thinks when we are mad at Him, especially knowing He was not the cause of the pain. I feel like He doesn't take it personally, just like I don't with my own kids And He is even more patient with us than I'd ever be. Another thing weighing on my mind was the fact that as a youth pastor and someone who put her trust in God, I felt guilty for feeling angry with Him. I kept asking myself if it was a sin to be mad at God? I don't believe having the *feelings* of anger are a sin, but I do believe if a person acts on those feelings by rejecting God or chooses to focus on the anger, it will eventually cause them to turn away from Him.

On August 20, 2004, one day before Judy's birthday, she lost her husband of 42 years. He was at home with his family surrounding him. The grief was unbearable. My sister-in-law, Joy, had a baby just a few weeks earlier. I tried to help with her much as I could in those first few days of utter gut-wrenching pain. Instead of it being about me this time, even though I was also hurting, I needed to support to my husband who had just lost his hero. I needed to be there for my boys, the oldest two hurting the most. Carter who was ten years old at the time was desperately in pain. Because he was the oldest grandchild, he had spent the most time with his grandpa, who was very involved in his life. It's almost impossible to explain death to a child, and Carter was taking it hard. The only thing worse than knowing your kids are hurting is not being able to do anything about it. As a mom, I felt helpless. I couldn't fix it. It wasn't like a boo-boo that I could kiss and make better.

The decision to be happy is one that has to be made continually in a lifetime. I had lost my dad, my nephew Hunter, and now my father-in-law within the span of four years. One Sunday morning, I was listening to a prominent preacher and heard him say something that has helped me ever since.

He said, "Every person needs an 'I don't understand file in his mind.' When things happen in your life that you can't explain, rather than lay the blame onto God, put it in that file folder of your mind." I've had to do this several times in my life, and it helps me remove the focus from the pain I'm experiencing. Knowing how I felt after losing my dad, I tried to use the same principles to deal with Myron's passing. Putting my trust in Jesus, talking to Him, and focusing on the positive was the only way for me to pick up my heart off the floor and keep going. I had four little ones to raise, a husband to support, and a new youth ministry to run. Remembering how much my dad loved me helped me to picture how much God loved me and that gave me the power to keep going. I was resilient, it had become a part of my DNA. I kept going, no matter what. *I was going to be a Grit Girl.*

> The decision to be happy is one that has to be made continually in a lifetime. I had lost my dad, my nephew Hunter, and now my father-in-law within the span of four years. One Sunday morning, I was listening to a prominent preacher and heard him say something that has helped me ever since. He said, "Every person needs an 'I don't understand file in his mind.'

A Grit Girl is DEFINED by RESILIENCE.

While you're not likely to forget the pain of losing a loved one, a significant relationship, or ending a career you enjoyed, you can choose to focus on the positive. At first, you may have to do it multiple times a day, but it will get easier. Resilience will give you the courage to choose happiness, the resolve to enjoy life, and it will help you to discover you already have what it takes to do both because *you are a grit girl.*

A Grit Girl is not defined by pain; she is defined by her resilience.

"He brought me up out of a horrible pit [of tumult and of destruction], out of the miry clay,

And He set my feet upon a rock, steadying my footsteps and establishing my path."

Psalm 40:2 The Amplified Translation

CHAPTER 6

DIGGING DEEP I

I'M AMAZED AT HOW FAST TIME PASSES. FROM 2004 WHEN MYRON passed to 2010, we were crazy busy with full-time ministry work as youth pastors while simultaneously trying to make our kids' schedules our priority. They were involved in sports, a lot of sports. With the four of them, we had football, basketball, baseball, volleyball, and fast-pitch softball players. Other than yearly family vacations to Wisconsin Dells, we barley had time to think about anything other than ministry and kids.

Jeff definitely wasn't giving enough thought to his health, even though he noticed some shortness of breath in late December 2010. It was getting progressively more difficult to breathe, and it became clear to all of us on the morning of January 5, 2011. He's a big guy in stature and presence, not overweight, standing a little taller than 6ft and solid. He's strong—one reason I was attracted to him. He worked out most mornings for many years, including holidays. Before Christmas that year, he started to feel different, his breathing more difficult than it should have been during his 45-minutes of cardio. He thought, like a lot of people might have, he was just feeling off because of overeating during the holidays. No matter what is bothering Jeff, when asked, he'll always say he's fine. He finally mentioned the shortness of breath to me, and after I bugged him for a few days, he scheduled an appointment for Friday January 6.

The morning of January 5, after walking up less than half a flight of stairs, he could hardly breathe. I insisted he be seen by a doctor *that* day. I hadn't noticed just how bad his breathing was until that moment. I wanted to go with him, but he was convinced it was no big deal and scheduled the appointment during his lunch hour. I anxiously waited for his call after seeing the doctor. I had been on the phone with my best friend, Anissa, asking her to pray for Jeff. She assured me everything was going to be fine. I then nodded off watching The Oprah Winfrey Show until the phone ringing woke me up just minutes later.

> The morning of January 5, after walking up less than half a flight of stairs, he could hardly breathe. I insisted he be seen by a doctor *that* day. I hadn't noticed just how bad his breathing was until that moment.

"They are sending me to Suburban Imaging for x-rays. Dr. Gu thinks I may have multiple blood clots in my lungs and he needs imaging to confirm." Jeff told me without an ounce of worry in his voice. I started to panic, "Clots? What does that mean?" He's always the calm one, and this conversation was no different. The clots explained his shortness of breath, and he assured me it sounded worse than it was, trying not to worry me. Again, all I could do was wait for another call after Jeff was done with his imaging appointment. I sat anxiously waiting to hear the x-rays results while trying to convince myself Jeff was right not to be worried. Less than an hour later, he called to tell me they were sending him to the hospital. Carter had a basketball game that night. In fact, it was parent night. Jeff asked his doctor if he I could go to the game before the hospital. I'm sure Dr. Gu thought he was crazy so, of course, said no. I told him I could be at the clinic within 15 minutes, so I could drive him, but he insisted on driving himself. My mind was racing, "The hospital? You're driving yourself there?" I said panicking. He continued trying to convince me it wasn't a big deal. He always puts the kids first and insisted I go to the game, participate in parent night with Carter, and come to the hospital afterward. I should have been making dinner for our other three kids, but I couldn't think straight, much less pull together a meal. I wandered around the house aimlessly for the next hour, sorting mail and doing laundry, basically keeping myself busy to pass the time until I could get to the game and eventually the hospital.

I planned my night as he suggested, attending the game with my mother-in-law, Judy, who rode with the kids and me, so she could come with me to the hospital. I wasn't able to talk to Carter or any of his coaches before the game to let them know what was going on with Jeff, and I knew Carter would immediately notice Jeff wasn't there. I worried the entire first half of the game that he wouldn't be able to concentrate once he noticed the open spot next to me. During half-time, the parents were called up front, each mom receiving a flower, and the players individually thanking their parents for their time and support. Carter made his way to me quickly, asking where his dad was, and knowing about his dad's shortness of breath and the appointment before school that morning. I whispered in his ear, trying not to alarm him, "He's in the hospital, but he's going to be okay. We're going to see him after the game." You can do only so much to keep your kids from being worried. As much as I tried to say it in a way not to upset him before playing the second half, there was no way to avoid it. I couldn't keep my eyes off the scoreboard, wishing the clock would count down quicker. I was not only watching Carter with the ball, but I was trying to read his face, knowing he was worried about Jeff. I prayed a little prayer that he'd be able to block out what was going on with Jeff and concentrate on the game. Like me, he spent the rest of the game looking at the clock—not for the score, but more for counting down the minutes when he could see his dad.

As soon as the game-ending buzzer rang, Judy, me and all four kids headed to Mercy Hospital, the same place my dad had passed away. *I hate that hospital.* We barely fit in Jeff's small room on the fourth floor, in the newly opened Heart Center wing. As always, he was positive, not surprising since he's never one to worry. He actually seemed more annoyed with the situation than upset, explaining how inconvenient it was and how much he had to do the next couple of days. By the time we got to the hospital that night, it as almost 9 pm, and with the kids needing to wake up early for school the next day, we weren't able to stay long. It was difficult for me to leave Jeff in the hospital, and even more difficult on the kids. We all gave him hugs and prayed together before we left. He was put on an IV of Heparin, which would thin the clots that filled his lungs. We were told he'd be in the hospital for two to three days, depending on how long it took for the clots to dissolve. Although I hated leaving him there alone, I didn't feel scared.

The following morning, I asked a friend to give the kids a ride to school. I pulled myself together and headed to the hospital to sit with Jeff. It was a Friday morning, and normally he would be with 5 or 6 friends who met weekly to discuss the Bible and have breakfast. Instead of attending the group, his friend Troy came to visit him at the hospital. Knowing Troy was with Jeff, I didn't particularly hurry that morning and arrived around 10:30 am. I walked into his room just in time to hear a doctor explain she had concerns about his heart, so they were scheduling an echocardiogram within the hour. He was given medication to relax during the test. Troy and I left and waited in the area outside the room. Judy arrived and the three of us chatted about meaningless news stories, trying to keep our thoughts from going elsewhere.

About 30 minutes later, we were brought back to the room to be given the results. Dr. O pointed to the screen, which looked similar to an ultrasound, and said, "Do you see this clot right here? It's sitting in a hole in Jeff's heart. Did you know Jeff had a hole in his heart?" Both Judy and I shook our heads no. "I've never seen this before, but this clot has moved through his right ventricle and is just sitting in the hole." He continued. "He could have sneezed or coughed, dislodging the clot. And if he had, it would have traveled to his left ventricle, causing a massive stroke and death." We were in shock. Jeff lied there, not saying a word, still slightly incoherent and drugged. I wasn't sure he was catching what the doctor was saying. Before I knew it, a world-renowned heart surgeon was standing in the room talking to us. He had a terrible bed-side manner, but his nurse was sweet and reassuring. "I've never seen anything like this before, not in all my years in practice." The nurse had her hand gently on my back. Restating his words with a more pleasant tone, he continued, "I could operate on him and he could die, or I could not operate on him, and he could have a massive stroke and die." He said matter-of-factly and then just stared at me. Dumbfounded, I asked, "So, are you asking me to decide?"

He quickly answered, "We don't operate on people unless they want us to." With Jeff still not 100% aware of his surroundings, I was making the decision on his behalf. I couldn't believe what I was hearing. I looked at Judy, then Troy, glanced at Jeff whose eyes were welling up with tears, and told the surgeon I didn't feel we had any choice but

> "I could operate on him and he could die, or I could not operate on him, and he could have a massive stroke and die." He said matter-of-factly and then just stared at me.

to go forward with emergency open heart surgery. I overheard a call being made to prep the operating room and my heart sank. Within minutes, they were wheeling Jeff out of the room and down the hall toward a set of silver double doors, the kind you see in movies, you're never allowed to enter. Just before he was out of sight, he handed me his wedding ring, saying, "I love you." I tried to be strong and not cry in front of him. It all happened so fast; I just stood there outside the doors, alone.

We were told the surgery would last a minimum of eight hours, maybe even nine. My pastor and his wife came to the hospital with two other pastors from our church. Jeff's siblings and my mom also arrived. We prayed, talked, and ate snacks to pass the time, all the while I was watching the electronic patient communication board like a hawk. There were important code words we were supposed to watch for that marked significant milestones of the surgery. I learned that OTP stood for 'on the pump,' meaning his heart was outside of his body, and it was pumping by a machine. OFP stood for 'off the pump,' signifying his heart was back in his body pumping on its own. OFP was the code to watch for because it also meant the surgery was nearing an end.

The entire day I was not only worried about Jeff, but also concerned about the kids. All four of them attended a small Christian school, on the same campus as the church where we worked. I was nervous that word of Jeff's emergency open heart surgery would make it to my kids inadvertently. I didn't want them to find out via hearsay; I wanted to be the one to tell them. I made arrangements throughout the day for each of them to go home after school with a friend, hoping they could have a fun night without worrying about their dad.

Carter was 16 and the only one not going to a friend's due to a late basketball practice. I asked my brother Tim to bring him up to the hospital after the surgery that night. My flawed thinking was if Carter was able to see him alive and breathing, it would settle any fear he had of his dad dying. He saw his dad after Jeff returned from post-op to his room an hour after surgery. Seeing his dad poked full of tubes, on a ventilator, and in terrible pain had the opposite effect I had hoped for. I had just made a huge mistake; he was traumatized. I saw his eyes widen and well up with tears, shocked by the number of monitors and tubes and the ventilator. I'm not sure what he was expecting, but that was not it. It was obvious Jeff was in an incredible amount of pain, having just had his entire chest cracked open, and he was moaning in pain and wasn't even aware Carter was standing there. Not only was I overwhelmed by the events of that day, but seeing the fear and tears in my son's eyes was also heartbreaking. I felt like a terrible mom.

Knowing I was exhausted, my mom offered to stay overnight at the hospital with Jeff. I thought that leaving him the night before was difficult, this felt like I was abandoning him. Since Jeff was not totally aware of who was in the room, I felt it was more important I go home to sleep, so I could function the next day and be there for him. I got home around 1 am; I can't explain how alone I felt in the dark house. I felt like wanting to explain to the house and even the dog what had happened to Jeff. Even though I was exhausted, I couldn't shut down my mind, replaying the same thoughts again and again: my husband almost died today, my husband could have died today, my husband should have died today. I eventually fell asleep in our bed, in my clothes, hugging his pillow.

Just two days after surgery, while a nurse was lowering Jeff back into his hospital bed, he was dropped roughly back into lying position. I saw his newly cracked-open chest jolt as he landed with a thud. I could see the pain in this face and the wince in his eyes. Within moments, alarms started to go off, and nurses and doctors rushed into the room as he began to signal that he was again having difficulty breathing. After x-rays they discovered another clot had traveled from his leg into his already full lungs. There simply wasn't enough room left in his lungs for air. That one extra clot sent him to ICU for three days. All I could think was *I have to be strong. I have to be his advocate. I need to be here for him.*

Just days after being released from ICU, Jeff was discharged. I was overwhelmed at the thought of running the household, managing the kids, and taking care of Jeff at the same time. For the first week, I slept on the floor by the bed, so I wouldn't disturb him during the night, not to mention the entire mattress was propped up for his chest to heal. I woke up every time he made a sound reminding me of having a newborn when as a mom you hear every breath they take. I tried my best to make him feel comfortable—whether with pain medication, switching positions, or rearranging pillows—anything to try to help alleviate the massive amount of pain he was in. I had to stay strong.

Our community of family, friends, and church were beyond amazing. The Bible talks about Jesus' grace being enough to see us through any situation, and I was able to experience this in a very tangible way. Grace isn't simply a concept or idea; it's often an action. Jeff and I had a community of friends that revolved around our church and ministry. These were the very people God used to deliver His grace to our family. They were the hands and feet of Jesus, surrounding us with the basics we needed to get through life with four kids while dealing with a major medical setback. Wonderful homemade meals came daily. People gave my kids rides and gift cards, so they could eat in between school and after school sports. My sister, mom, in-laws, and friends came to the house and did laundry and cleaned in order to lighten my workload. One family even paid for a plow service every time it snowed, which in Minnesota is a lot! It felt like I was getting a God-hug every single day. I had always been on the giving end of support, but never the receiving end, and it was so beautiful to see and feel the love and support of so many.

About two weeks into Jeff's recovery, he started to complain about pain in his chest. Even though he just had emergency open heart surgery for shortness of breath, he refused to go to the hospital that night, instead waiting for his scheduled appointment the next day. By the time we arrived at the hospital the next morning, Jeff was nearly gray and could barely walk. It was so bad that I had to get him a wheelchair. When the surgeon saw Jeff, he was furious. He could tell just by looking at him that his blood was too thin. He knew somebody somewhere had given us bad information. After his heart surgery, Jeff was put on Warfarin, a drug used to thin the blood, mainly the clots in his lungs. Because most patients do not know their INR baseline, the dosage has to be monitored in order to determine the proper prescription. When patients begin taking Warfarin, they must go to the clinic every day in order to test their blood to determine the perfect dosage based on their INR levels. We were unfamiliar with blood thinners, INR levels—really, all of it. Up until this point, Jeff had never experienced any sort of medical problems. We were told we did not need to come in over the weekend to check his INR.

He was re-admitted to the fourth-floor heart unit; a place I never expected to be in, especially twice. He was barely in his hospital bed when they wheeled him out for x-ray. I sat there, alone in his room, my mind racing. I was half praying and half talking to God, "This has to be okay. This nightmare has to be over; please, no more." Jeff and the doctor returned rather quickly. The doc had the x-rays in his hand. He explained that Jeff was bleeding internally and had the equivalent liquid of a two-liter of soda around his heart. "He should have had a massive heart attack and died," Dr. O said, shaking his head. "That's twice this guy should have died." Looking at Jeff, "He's one lucky guy!" I couldn't help myself and quickly told him, "He's not lucky; it's God's mercy that kept him alive, for the second time." I had just received a massive God-hug, He saved my husband's life—not once—but twice!

My friends and family continued to offer massive support after Jeff was discharged for the second time. He would need to spend the next few months recovering and attending physical therapy. The only nice thing about the hospital was that they were responsible for his care—*not me*. I wanted my normal life back; I wanted Jeff back. I'm not complaining, not by a long shot, however, Jeff's near-death experiences had turned our lives upside down. Suddenly, I was in charge of the kids' schedule including the 30-minute drive to and from school every day and keeping up with their crazy schedules of sports. I was also driving Jeff to the clinic every morning to monitor his INR levels—in general, I was responsible for keeping track of everything and everyone. Emotionally, I was exhausted trying to be strong for Jeff and the kids. I had zero alone time, and honestly I do best when I have quiet time to myself. To top it all off, even though I knew Jesus was there and His grace was working in our lives, I was too tired to connect with Him, spending no time reading my Bible or praying. Jeff couldn't attend church the first few weeks, so I wasn't able to do that either. I learned it's in those times, when I feel the most disconnected from Jesus, that His grace is picking up my slack. Several people asked me why God allowed this to happen, and my answer is always the same: I've resigned to file this in my mind in what I refer to as my 'I don't understand file.' I don't know why, but I do know He protected Jeff long enough to get to a doctor who knew what to do. Because of this, his life was spared.

> Grit got me through those six months, from the day Jeff was admitted to the hospital to the day he was considered fully recovered.

Grit got me through those six months, from the day Jeff was admitted to the hospital to the day he was considered fully recovered. Being strong didn't make my life perfect by a long shot, but that resiliency helped me to make it through. On difficult days, I had to remind myself continually, *you can do this.*

A Grit Girl is <u>DEFINED</u> by <u>RESILIENCE.</u>

We often feel ill-prepared to handle the storms we face, and it's in those times that we need to remember we aren't facing them alone, nor are we responsible to fix them. When we choose to put our trust in Jesus, His grace carries us through, whether we are alone or have an army of help. A grit girl is humble, and her resilient spirit is willing to ask for help when necessary because true strength isn't afraid to express need. Asking for help is not a sign of weakness; it's a sign you are willing to do what it takes to improve your situation—you'll push through because you are defined by resilience. *You are a Grit Girl.*

"The LORD is my rock, my fortress, and the One who rescues me; My God, my rock and strength in whom I trust and take refuge; My shield, and the horn of my salvation, my high tower—my stronghold."

Psalm 18:3 The Amplified Bible

CHAPTER 7

DIGGING DEEP II

IT WAS A RARE FRIDAY NIGHT WITHOUT ANY PLANNED ACTIVITIES OR KIDS' games. Jeff and I were at home watching Dateline when I reached under my left bra strap to scratch an itch. I felt a little lump as if, somehow, a small marble were under my skin. My first thought was *that's weird, but I'm sure it's nothing*. I kept feeling it, trying to convince myself it was nothing—it's nothing, it's nothing. My thought immediately took me to my annual physical from the year before. My primary doctor had strongly suggested I get a mammogram when I turned 40. I was more than a year behind in having it done. I debated about saying anything to Jeff, thinking and hoping it was nothing. I couldn't keep it to myself, so I told him, trying to convince myself by convincing him that it was just an odd bump. That night when we went to bed, I laid flat on my back and felt for it, but I couldn't find anything. I tried reassuring myself *see, you were starting to freak out for no reason; it's not even there anymore*. Moments later I sat straight up in bed to double check—yep, still there. I tried my best to put it out of my mind knowing there was nothing I could do anyways. The first thing I did when I woke up the next morning was the last thing I did before bed. I felt for the marble—lying down, sitting up, standing up, in the shower. *It was still there.*

The following evening we spent the night with close friends, Troy and Tia. Tia had battled breast cancer a few years earlier, so I knew if anyone could help me, she'd be able to tell me whether or not I was overthinking what I had discovered. While the guys watched a football game, Tia and I ran to the grocery store to pick up dessert when I blurted out, "I found something. I'm not sure what it is. Can you feel it?" She felt the marble lump while we were sitting in the parking lot deciding on brownies or cheesecake. Tia has a calming presence, never one to overreact. She simply said, "I think you should get it checked." The words hung over my head, even though I tried to ignore them. I told myself, *All I need to do is make it to Monday. I just need to see my nurse practitioner, and she'll tell me it's nothing—just two more days.*

> "I found something. I'm not sure what it is. Can you feel it?" She felt the marble lump while we were sitting in the parking lot deciding on brownies or cheesecake. Tia has a calming presence, never one to overreact. She simply said, "I think you should get it checked."

That weekend I hosted Easter Sunday dinner for my side of the family. That year Easter happened to fall the Sunday before Brock and my mom's birthday—April 11. We decided to celebrate both birthdays the same afternoon after dinner. It was a weird day. I can't really explain why it felt weird; it was like everybody was 'off.' Maybe I was the only one truly out of sorts, so that may have made me feel like it was everyone else too. I'm not really sure. We were celebrating Brocks 16th, and I didn't want to seem distracted so I tried to do my best to ignore my racing thoughts and make the day nice for him.. Monday couldn't come soon enough.

I was at the doctor's office for the earliest appointment available at 10 am to see my nurse practitioner, Jen. She was always kind, gentle, and never one to make the appointment feel rushed. She gave me a routine breast exam and felt the lump and the surrounding lymph nodes under my arms. Even though she tried her hardest to make me feel at ease, I could tell by the look on her face that she was concerned. Trying to calm my nerves she said, "It could just be a cyst or just a fatty deposit. We should get it checked out by a radiologist just to make sure." She momentarily left the room to schedule an appointment at the Specialty Breast Care Center. I was amazed that they responded to her rather quickly with an opening for the following morning. While I was relieved I didn't have to wait for days to have the ultrasound, it was a bit worrisome that they were getting me in so fast. I left my appointment more worried than when I had arrived. My mind racing, I thought *Do they know something already that I don't know? Will an ultrasound tell me if I have breast cancer?* The questions in my head were non-stop.

The appointment at the Breast Care Center was Tuesday morning, just four days after I'd discovered the lump. That day I just so happened to be working on a painting project at a friend's house not too far from the clinic. Since I was going to be at her house before and possibly even after the appointment, I insisted Jeff stay at the office, assuring him I'd update him immediately afterward. Jeff was 100% willing to meet me there, always supportive and willing to drop everything at the office to be with me when I needed him. I convinced him I would be fine going by myself, hoping I'd be able to call him afterward to report this was just a false alarm.

The first part of my appointment was spent on a mammogram, which I was supposed to have done the year before. I was brought into a small locker room type space and asked to put on a gown, opened at the front. I didn't know it, *but I was going to get accustomed to these hospital gowns.* I had no idea what to expect from the mammogram, thinking it was going to be similar to an x-ray. The only way it was like an x-ray was the picture part—the rest, not so much. They squished, pulled, and prodded my breasts every way imaginable. I didn't know the girls could get that flat or stretch that far—WOW. Next, I was sent to an ultrasound room to have a technician take ultrasound pictures—totally painless and over quickly. When the technician was finished, she told me to wait on the table while she took the information to the radiologist, who would read the results on the spot. When she left the room, I again thought

Does she know something I don't know? What did she see? Do they have everyone stay and wait on the table? Why did I insist on coming to this appointment alone? I feel painfully alone. After only a few minutes, the radiologist returned and sat down next to me. He told me I had a small mass visible on the reading and suggested an ultrasound biopsy on the spot. After having the nurse numb the area, he returned with giant syringe-looking needle, explaining the needle has a small device on the end that he would basically shoot into my breast and grab a chunk of tissue; it would be a little painful, but they'd give me an ice pack afterward. More questions: *A piece of tissue? Do you mean a piece of my breast? This big needle thing is grabbing something and ripping it out of my body?* It really wasn't as bad as I was anticipating, over in less than fifteen minutes. After getting dressed, I met with a nurse in a small office where I got a small round ice pack and told someone would call in the next few days with results. I walked out to my car, knowing I had to drive back to my friend's house to finish our painting project. Stacy and I were friends because our kids attended the same school, but I didn't know her very well at the time. I could have shared with her what was going on and probably should have. I know she would have hugged me and prayed for me. And although I was exploding with something to say on the inside, I left that day without mentioning the lump, the Breast Center, or the biopsy.

The next morning was Wednesday, five days after finding the lump. I drove to a local pole barn where my sister Kelsey, sister-in-law Jennifer, and I had a make-shift paint station set up. We'd started a business re-purposing furniture and selling it in a local antique shop. Using paint sprayers was always a bit tricky, so we often carefully planned the color we would be using and how many pieces of furniture we could finish before having to switch colors in the sprayer. That day we were painting with a trendy aqua blue. The barn was filled with a faint blue mist of paint, almost like a thin fog. I was hoping to receive a call that day, even though the day before the nurse told me it would be anywhere from one to three days. I thought maybe if I had my phone handy, I could will them into calling that day. I kept my phone close, anxiously waiting, while pretending I wasn't consumed with crazy thoughts and fear. Glancing over at my phone, I see the two words I did not want to see most—missed call. *I couldn't believe it.* I grabbed the phone and went outside to sit in what I called my mom-van to return the call. I got a voicemail system. "Are you kidding me?" I said out loud to myself. I decided I'd just sit there and wait for another call back. I was not going to miss it a second time. It was hot for April, and my vehicle was sitting in the direct sun. I hate being hot, so I put the windows down, hoping for some fresh air. The fresh air turned out to be not so fresh. I was parked just a few feet from a herd of cows. To this day, the smell of manure brings me right back to this moment.

After an agonizing ten-minute wait, my cell phone rang. The caller ID read CLINIC. I took a deep breath and answered, "This is Sunday." There was a sweet woman on the other end who sounded exactly how I remembered my Grandmother sounding, "We have your test results back, and I'm so sorry to tell you that you have Invasive Ductile Carcinoma." Although I had a feeling that's what the results would be, hearing the actual words was something I don't think anyone can prepare you for. My response was short, "Okay." She continued, "Do you understand what I am telling you, honey? You have breast cancer." The words just hung in the air somewhere between her phone and mine: You have breast cancer. Again, I replied with a simple, "Okay." I'm sure she'd experienced similar responses, or maybe not, so she tried to make sure I was hearing what she was saying. She continued by asking if I'd like her to spell it for me. I declined. I didn't need her to spell it; I fully understood *that I had breast cancer.*

> I took a deep breath and answered, "This is Sunday." There was a sweet woman on the other end who sounded exactly how I remembered my Grandmother sounding, "We have your test results back, and I'm so sorry to tell you that you have Invasive Ductile Carcinoma."

I sat there in my mom-van, stunned, tears running down my cheeks. All I could think was *I can't have cancer. I have four kids. I have four kids.* My hands were shaking as I scrolled through the recent calls on my cell phone until I found my husband's name: ICE Honey. When he answered, he immediately knew something was wrong because he knew I was on the other end, yet no words were coming out of my mouth. I was crying so hard I couldn't get out a single word. Eventually, I got the words out, "They said I have breast cancer." His response wasn't surprising: "Everything is going to be okay." Classic response, always brave, always strong, and, most importantly, always calm. My mind was racing. I couldn't imagine how everything was going to be okay. Regardless, his words did make me feel better. We decided Jeff would stay at work. Coming home wouldn't change anything, and we'd let the kids continue with their afterschool activities without mentioning the awful words that had suddenly become a part of who I was.

After crying and yelling at no one in the car, I fumbled through the contacts on my phone to once again find MOM!—exactly how I have her saved in my phone. She wasn't near as calm as Jeff. My mom and I cried together as she started asking questions. I had zero answers. We talked about how we both knew Jesus would be there with me every step of the way. After a good cry, we prayed together through our tears and ended the call with her unknowingly saying the same thing Jeff had: "Everything is going to be okay."

> All I could think was *I can't have cancer. I have four kids. I have four kids.* My hands were shaking as I scrolled through the recent calls on my cell phone until I found my husband's name: ICE Honey. When he answered, he immediately knew something was wrong because he knew I was on the other end, yet no words were coming out of my mouth.

I momentarily forgot I was sitting in my car, on a farm, outside of a pole barn. My sisters were still inside painting, and I had no choice but to go back in and deliver the news. I opened the barn door and walked through the aqua blue mist, making my way to the back corner where we were painting. My sisters, who heard the door open, stopped the sprayers and waited for me to walk by the tractors, the furniture, and through the blue fog. It felt like forever to get to them and when I did, they were standing with sprayers in hand and their paint masks slightly pulled down off their faces. I didn't say a word.

I didn't have to. As soon as I saw them, I just stopped, tears running down my cheeks, nodding my head yes. We stood there hugging and crying together. I didn't know what to do next, so I just drove home, alone.

There was only one thing on my mind during the 10-minute drive home. It was Carter, Brock, Tucker, and Kennedy. My thoughts quickly shifted from flight to fight. I decided in that moment that I would do everything possible to beat the cancer, refusing to leave my kids without a mom. I knew I was a fighter and was going to do whatever it took to survive. I needed to put my trust in Jesus more than I ever had before, and I needed to depend on His grace in a way I hadn't in the past. I knew I was resilient, but now I was going to have to prove it to myself. I decided right then that I would recover from cancer, and I would continue with my most important job—mom.

On April 11, 2012, the day I was diagnosed with breast cancer, I chose to be a Grit Girl.

A Grit Girl is DEFINED by RESILIENCE.

Hearing the words "You have breast cancer" felt like a punch in the gut. They say once you've been diagnosed, you often split your life in two: before cancer and after cancer. I knew right away I didn't want to be just a breast cancer survivor—cancer is only part of my story. I choose to be defined by resilience, not my setback. And you can do the same *because I am a Grit Girl and so are you.*

"When the righteous cry for help, the LORD hears and delivers them out of all their troubles. The LORD is near to the brokenhearted and saves the crushed in spirit. Many are the afflictions of the righteous, but the LORD delivers him out of them all."

Psalm 34:17–19 The English Standard Version

CHAPTER 8
SURGERY, STRENGTH & SUPPORT

I HAD NO IDEA WHAT CANCER HAD IN STORE FOR ME. I HAD NEVER RE-
ally given the clinical or practical side of cancer much thought. I had
obviously experienced the loss and seen the suffering first-hand, but
facing it as my diagnosis, my treatment, *my cancer* was an entirely
different story. I had never considered the amount of appointments,
doctors, and decisions my dad and Myron had to make. I was completely unaware of the impact of the number of choices, options, and
opinions had on a person. My diagnosis alone was enough to make
my head spin, let alone having to think clearly enough to make decisions that would effect my life. I had to get quiet. I had to sit alone
and cry out to Jesus. I had to tell Him that I needed Him; I needed
grace to face what was coming in the months ahead. When I went
to bed at night, I played a CD of Bible verse readings, leaving it on
repeat the entire night. Those scriptures brought so much peace into
a situation that felt anything but peaceful. In the upcoming weeks,

I would have to choose a surgeon, a plastic surgeon, an oncologist, a hospital, a clinic, and eventually a radiologist—all while trying to keep it somewhat together emotionally. The Monday after receiving the devastating call, *the crazy began.*

One thing I noticed as soon as my friends and family found out about my diagnosis was that certain people were full of advice—whether I asked for it or not. One of the most particularly amusing pieces of advice I received was from an older friend who suggested, "You should just go off sugar for six months and see what happens." I was outwardly gracious. But inside, I was screaming *Are you crazy? I have four kids. I can't wait six months to see what happens!* I can laugh about it now because I realize people are well-meaning, yet completely ill-informed. On the other hand, having the opportunity to talk to someone who had recently been through breast cancer meant the world to me.

It wasn't long before I realized I'd be moved into a position where my breasts would literally hang down through the opening while the technician examined them—hanging through a hole, not covered, cold, and extremely awkward. *No wonder they offered me Valium!* During the exam, I had to repeatedly tell myself *Breathe, you can breathe, you are fine, just relax. It will be over soon, you can breathe.*

Less than a week after my diagnosis, I was put in touch with a pastor who had been diagnosed just a couple of years prior. This woman was extremely busy, yet she took the time to speak with me on the phone for more than an hour. I'll never forget receiving the call that day. I was in a floral shop ordering a corsage for my son's prom date when she called. I totally ignored the fact I was in a store, pulling up a chair from a wrought iron bistro set in which the florist most likely did her consolations. It's weird, but the one thing I remember most about our conversation was how wonderful the flowers around me smelled—at least, that was better than the smell of cows. We discussed implants, drainage tubes, chemo, and prayer all in the same conversation. Not only did she answer all the questions I could think of, she sent periodic texts and kept in touch for almost a full year. I cannot explain how much that meant to me. Even though I was getting unsolicited advice, I was receiving more love and support than I could have imagined while I anxiously waited for my first official doctor's appointment after learning about the cancer.

Before I could meet with a doctor for a detailed diagnosis and treatment options, I was asked to schedule an MRI in order to have complete information regarding the size of the tumor and to detect if there were any others. The MRI was scheduled at Mercy Hospital, same place where my dad died and where Jeff's life was saved. I *really* didn't want to go there, but I had no choice. I wasn't sure why, but I was required to bring a driver with me to the appointment, so I brought my mom. After checking in, I was again asked to change into a gown, open to the front, and told to wait in a small waiting area. After a few moments, the nurse collected and lead us back to the MRI area—it was so cold back there! Once in the room, the nurse asked if I'd like a Valium to calm my nerves. Now I knew why I needed a driver. My response, "Can I have two?" I have a tendency toward claustrophobia, so I tried to occupy my mind by talking to my mom about things that didn't matter, even laughing about the hairnet they made me wear. I thought the longer I didn't think about that small, trapped space that I had to lie completely still in, the more mentally prepared I'd be. I was hoping the Valium would help me not to hyperventilate. I was told to lie on my stomach, and I remember thinking the request was odd—until I saw a large opening where I was to lie, face down. It wasn't long before I realized I'd be moved into a position where my breasts would literally hang down through the opening while the technician examined them—hanging through a hole, not covered, cold, and extremely awkward. *No wonder they offered me Valium!* During the exam, I had to repeatedly tell myself *Breathe, you can breathe, you are fine, just relax. It will be over soon, you can breathe.* I was in this giant tube for little more than 30 minutes before the slow-moving machine had me out. Although it was uncomfortable, even borderline embarrassing, the MRI provided valuable information regarding the size of the tumor I had found and now a previously undetected tumor. Had I scheduled my mammogram a year earlier when my doctor asked, both tumors could have been discovered—at a smaller stage. I'll never know if this would have changed the outcome of my surgeries and treatment, but I'm just grateful I found the lump when I did. I consider finding my lump another God-hug. I felt a little tipsy while getting re-dressed, so it was a good thing my mom was there. I was in no condition to drive. Not only that, but I was also happy to have my mom's moral support. Sometimes, you just need your mom to be there for you when your girl parts are on display. That day, we had a great laugh about the entire appointment on the way home.

The MRI results were sent to my surgeon before my first appointment. He was an older man, nearing the end of his surgical career. It was evident he had cared for thousands of women just like me—the appointment felt routine and cold. He briefly explained the process he felt was best for my situation. Finding the second tumor in my left breast ruled out a lumpectomy, which is the removal of just the tumor and a small surrounding area. My options were to decide between a single or double mastectomy and reconstruction. He explained that he also needed to do a biopsy of my lymph nodes to see if the cancer had spread. This could only be done during the mastectomy. I had never heard of a bi-lateral lymph node dissection, but I now know it's very common for women undergoing surgery to remove breast cancer. My memory is now fuzzy when I think back to that first appointment as if I tried to block it out. Jeff and I listened to about 30 minutes of clinical information, the official diagnosis, recommendations, and treatment options. It all felt like a foreign language to me. I sat there half listening and half staring blankly at the self-breast exam posters on the wall in his office. I thought to myself *I should have done that*. I was grateful to have Jeff with me; he's my emotional support and my rock.

We had waited to tell the kids about the diagnosis until after this appointment in order to have answers about treatment. I felt it would be harder on them to hear the report and then leave them wondering what would happen next. I had been dreading this day—the day I had to tell my kids they had *another* parent facing a life-threatening situation. The absolute worst part of my breast cancer diagnosis was telling my kids. They were 12, 14, 16, and 18 and had just barely emotionally worked through the near death of their dad a year earlier. I tried to convince my husband we didn't have to tell them, that we could keep it a secret. I was doing my best to convince myself to believe a lie, that I could protect them from this and any other difficult life situation. That night we sat them down together for a family meeting. Right away, the kids knew it wasn't going to be good; we rarely had official family meetings. Jeff and I are more of the "teach as you go and lead by example" types, so an official sit-down with all four kids was unusual for us. I tried my hardest not to cry and to appear strong while Jeff told the kids their mom had been diagnosed with breast cancer. They were in complete shock, having no idea what we had gone through the past two weeks. I'll never forget the image of Carter, sitting across the living room in a blue accent chair, putting his head in his hands and sobbing; *it was heartbreaking*. As difficult as it was and as much as I wanted to protect them from the fear of losing me, I knew I had been presented with a unique opportunity. I was determined not only to fight for my complete recovery, but also to do it in a way that demonstrated a combination of authenticity and strength—you could say, my grit. I refused to feel sorry for myself or allow them to see me scared. Although I, of course, was scared, I knew if they saw fear in my eyes, then it would magnify how afraid they were already feeling. My goal was to be an example of a woman full of strength who refused to give up while at the same time vulnerable enough for them to understand that my weaknesses *were okay too*. The struggle was with my humanity; my strength came from the only person bigger than my humanness. The grace to make it through would come only from my dependence on Jesus. In most cases, a child or even a teenager is not able to verbalize what they are observing in the life of their parents; however, they are like sponges, absorbing everything we do, even more than what we say. The words my mom and Jeff said to me within minutes of hearing my diagnoses were the exact words I used to try to comfort all four of my children: "Everything is going to be okay."

> Finding the second tumor in my left breast ruled out a lumpectomy, which is the removal of just the tumor and a small surrounding area. My options were to decide between a single or double mastectomy and reconstruction.

My second important appointment was with a plastic surgeon. I was so overwhelmed by the entire situation that I went to the first doctor my surgeon recommended. Kelsey, my younger sister, was my constant support system and accompanied me to the appointment. I immediately liked my doctor; he's calming, soft-spoken, and has a caring way about him. After discussing options and looking at before and after photos, we discussed my expectations and his expertise. He made it abundantly clear that his first priority was to make sure I was cancer free. Second, he would do everything possible for me to feel good about how I looked. At the time, I didn't have a grasp on how difficult losing such an intimate part of my body would be. Seeing the photos of the women who'd already had surgery made it start to feel real.

> I chose a double mastectomy. My biggest reason was that after reconstruction, the impacted breast would have a certain look that would not change. Knowing that my body changes all the time, I was concerned my right side would change while my left would not.

One of the biggest decisions I had to make was deciding between a single or a double mastectomy. Because both tumors were found in the left breast, I didn't have to do a double if I didn't want to. This was something I had already talked through with my pastor friend. In fact, it was one of the first questions I had for her. It's amazing that the more women I talk to the more options I learn about. I find it interesting hearing the decisions other breast cancer survivors made—but more important, why. I made a decision before even meeting my plastic surgeon. I chose a double mastectomy. My biggest reason was that after reconstruction, the impacted breast would have a certain look that would not change. Knowing that my body changes all the time, I was concerned my right side would change while my left would not. And even though my second reason was the thought of reoccurrence, I gave greater consideration to having matching breasts.

During the majority of our visit, we discussed the types of reconstruction options available. In my case, I had two main options: a trans-flap surgery or implants. A trans-flap, which I'd never heard of before now, involved using belly fat tissue to re-create the breasts. Although it involves a longer recovery time, the idea sounded much like a tummy-tuck, which I was all about. In order to evaluate if I qualified for the trans-flap surgery, which was based on the amount of fat I had, my plastic surgeon had to roughly measure how much belly fat I had. The following is my most embarrassing moment ever—*like ever*. I had to unzip my jeans, pull them slightly down, and stand in front of him while he squeezed my dreaded middle area. Meanwhile, Kelsey was sitting in the corner of the room laughing, which got me laughing. And by the time he finished giving my tummy fat a good squeeze, we were both crying from laughing so hard. Turns out, I didn't have enough fat for a trans-flap—God-hug—so the decision for implants was made for me. At the end of the appointment, my doctor offered to pray for me. The three of us held hands for a quick prayer. *I knew I liked this guy.*

A nurse called to set up a date for the nine-hour surgery that included a double mastectomy, lymph node dissection, and phase one reconstruction. It was less than a month from the day of my diagnosis. It felt like everything was moving so fast with the surgery set for May 1, 2012. I kept looking at myself in the mirror. I even had my sister snap a few photos, knowing my body would be forever changed. I haven't heard many women talk about this part of their cancer story, yet I know how devastating it feels. It's one thing to have plastic surgery because you *want* to, it's another because you *have* to. I hardly remember the three weeks between diagnosis and surgery. I know I had multiple doctor appointments and that I tried to busy myself so that I wouldn't think about it too much. I kept reassuring myself that I'd already experienced difficult situations and like the other times, I'd find the strength to push through.

Surgery day came faster than I expected. Before I knew it, I was up bright and early ready to head to the hospital. I wasn't allowed to wear make-up, but I curled my hair, hoping it would last a few days. I had to be to the hospital by 7am to check-in and was blessed to be accompanied by Jeff, my mom, my sister and three of my best friends. They were even wearing T-shirts in my honor. I've never felt so loved. After registration, I was taken to change and get my vitals checked. Thankfully, Jeff could be with me during my initial prep. I answered what felt like hundreds of questions and then got dressed for surgery. I dreaded the moment he was forced to leave for the waiting room once I was moved to pre-op, and we both cried as he went through the doors to the lobby. Being separated felt eerily similar to the day I watched him go through the double doors in the same hospital for his emergency open heart surgery. I felt so alone in my hospital bed, in between walls made of curtains, just a number in the long list of people lined up for surgery that day. Once I was situated, both my surgeon and my plastic surgeon came in to confirm exactly what would take place once I was in surgery. I laid flat on my back as they drew lines on my chest with a purple marker, talking about how they would work together. It was almost as if I wasn't even there. After the conversation, my surgeon left to get scrubbed in, but my plastic surgeon stayed behind to talk with me. I laid there with tears rolling down both cheeks. Trying to get a smile out of me, he asked, "Should we pray?" I nodded my head yes; who doesn't want prayer right before surgery? He answered his own question with, "Your turn!" I giggled—goal accomplished. I said a short prayer for him. With tears still filling my eyes, I was wheeled into surgery. Before long I was out.

Thankfully, there were no complications during the nine-hour triple surgery. Afterwards, both surgeons headed to the waiting room to talk to Jeff. While they were extremely reassuring, they informed him that they found cancer in my lymph nodes, removing 23. Finding cancer in the lymph nodes sounded scary, but they were confident they got all of it. Everyone was still waiting with Jeff, even after all these hours. He made the decision not to tell me that evening. "Let's let her recover tonight and I'll tell her tomorrow," they all agreed.

My best friend, Anissa, came up to my room to say goodbye, even though I was still extremely drugged up. In fact, our conversation is fuzzy to me, but not to her. She held my hand and told me she was going to head home, fully intending not to mention the cancer in my lymph nodes. Apparently, I opened my eyes as if I were fully aware of my surroundings, looked up at her and said, "They found it in my lymph nodes, didn't they?" Anissa cannot lie to save her life, and her reaction was typical. She just smiled back at me and said, "I love you." My response may be surprising to some, but I clearly said,

"Well, that's okay," and fell immediately back to sleep. The reason I was able to reply without panic was because even though I was not totally awake, in my heart of hearts I wasn't worried. *I was at peace.*

After spending the day at the hospital, Jeff needed to go to work the next day, so my mom and sister stayed overnight with me. I laid flat on my back the entire night, my chest wrapped like a mummy. My mom says I was groaning on and off in pain all night. The next morning my nurse greeted me with a frightening announcement. She told me I had to sit up, get out of bed, and go for a walk. I remember thinking *Are you nuts?* I was in so much pain, I thought for sure it wasn't possible to sit up after having my chest completely ripped apart. Turns out, the nurse was right—shocker. She slowly helped me sit and then stand up.

The short walk down the hall felt like a half marathon, even though it was literally down a short hallway and back. I was walking methodically as the two nurses made sure I was steady and cheered me on to finish the walk.

> The next morning my nurse greeted me with a frightening announcement. She told me I had to sit up, get out of bed, and go for a walk. I remember thinking *Are you nuts?* I was in so much pain, I thought for sure it wasn't possible to sit up after having my chest completely ripped apart.

Part of the reason I was in no rush to get back was because I knew what was next. Once we were back in the room, the nurse was going to change my dressing. I wasn't ready to see what my body looked like. I wasn't exactly sure when I'd be ready. I just could not look, yet.

My mom agreed to watch while they slowly unwrapped me. She was nervous for me, not really wanting to look either, but she was willing to do it for me. I was watching her face to see her reaction and she knew it. She tried hard not to react, and she did a good job. She looked right at me and reassured me it wasn't *that* bad, encouraging me to look in the mirror the next time they changed the dressings. I think I decided to look on the next change later that afternoon. I took a deep breath, let the nurse unwrap me most of the way, then with help stood in the bathroom alone to look. Basically, I was black and blue with scars that looked like a sideways letter Y coming across each breast. I could see the purple marker outlines, too. I don't think I cried. I actually didn't have a reaction; I just stared because I was simply numb to it all. There wasn't much I could do about it anyway.

I was exhausted and in pain, even though I took full advantage of the maximum amount of pain medication I was allowed to take. My kids stopped by to visit some mornings before school. They especially loved it because Jeff would treat them to Starbucks, and they had a great excuse to be late. They could visit in the afternoons only if there wasn't a conflict with baseball or softball. My two favorite photos from my time in the hospital are with my kids; one is a picture of Kennedy painting my toenails, the second is Carter and Brock kissing my cheeks—I didn't even care that I made them take it. Plenty of plants and flowers were delivered to the hospital, which were pretty to look at and smell. My favorite deliveries though were the cookie bouquets. I shared them with the kids, even though secretly I didn't want to. In fact, I may or may not have hid some of them. One evening all of my siblings came to visit at the same time, even though my room wasn't big enough for my three brothers, sister, and mom, I remember feeling hot, out of sorts, and tired. While I was thankful for the gesture, on the inside I just wanted them to leave, but I couldn't say so. My aunt Stephanie, who I affectionately call Teppe, brought me a little stuffed Grover from the children's TV show Sesame Street that I absolutely loved. Another favorite photo is of me holding up my Grover. I'm not sure why, but he made me happy. Up until this point, only a handful of people knew I'd been diagnosed, which helped with limiting the number of visitors. Everyone who did come asked the same questions. That is to be expected. How does one really know what to say in this type of situation? Never wanting to be a downer, I'd try to make light of the situation and point out the positives. I'd even joke about my silver lining being the plastic surgery that so many women dream

> My two favorite photos from my time in the hospital are with my kids; one is a picture of Kennedy painting my toenails, the second is Carter and Brock kissing my cheeks—I didn't even care that I made them take it.

of having, but never actually get. I used to think being the hospital was 'forced rest' and in one way it is; however, I learned quickly that you hardly get any rest in a hospital. Even though I was surprised to find out I would be in the hospital four days only—especially since I felt like I'd been hit with a Mack truck—I was happy to get home for *real* rest.

I was nervous about caring for myself at home, especially because I was going home with four drainage tubes hanging out of my sides. Imagine tubes with little bulbs on the ends literally hanging out of a hole on your body. *It was the weirdest feeling ever.* I had to be careful they didn't catch on anything, or they'd start to pull out. My sister and I tried using everything we could think of to hold them in place. She finally found a tube top shirt from Walmart that we put around my waist and tucked the bulbs into. Not only that, but because the tubes were draining excess fluid, I had to measure the amount of fluid in all four bulbs every few hours. It was a nightmare. I was still in pain and on medication, walking like an old lady, when I was forced to get up and move around. Once again, my sister was my rock, bringing healthy food and supplements to speed up my recovery. She even had to help me take a bath—*another laughing-until-we-cried moment for the two of us.*

A Grit Girl is DESTINED to be INSPIRING.

Your life is like a movie, a series of scenes creating the story of you. Every setback you face is just one scene in your story, not your entire story. You will make it from one scene to the next and when you look back, you'll realize the scenes in your story could have life-changing impact on someone else. You are destined to be inspiring, no matter the storm you face *because you are a Grit Girl.*

"And we know [with great confidence] that God [who is deeply concerned about us] causes all things to work together [as a plan] for good for those who love God, to those who are called according to His plan and purpose."

Romans 8:28 The Amplified Translation

CHAPTER 9

CHEMO, COLD-CAP & CARTER

SURGERY WAS THE FIRST STEP OF MANY IN THE LONG TREATMENT PROCESS. Next was chemotherapy. Before attending my first appointment with an oncologist, I was encouraged to attend a hospital provided class about chemotherapy. Although I didn't particularly feel like going to the class, I knew the information would be helpful. The day of the class I was nervous; I'm not sure why. Maybe I just didn't want to hear about all the negatives coming my way. I walked into the class last in the group, and not only were they giving me a stern 'you are late' look, but also they were all about 20 years older than I was. The class had no teacher or medical professional present. Basically, someone said welcome to class, and we watched a video. I was bored.

I was so distracted by everything around me that I wasn't even paying attention to the video with valuable information about nausea and constipation—now I really felt old! It was the words 'cold cap therapy' that got my attention. A brief description suggested it as an option for women going through chemotherapy, explaining it could greatly decrease the amount of hair loss during treatment. After class, I quickly Googled the term to get more information. I found a company called Penguin Cold Cap, which provides the therapy not covered by insurance. It involves renting frozen caps that are put on your head during chemo. The result is 75% less hair loss. Cold cap therapy, at the time, was relatively unknown and difficult to arrange. First, it's not covered by insurance and has a $3,000 price tag. Second, it is to be used only at a clinic housing a specific $5,000 cold cap freezer. Lastly, it requires an oncologist supportive of the therapy. I had a short window of two to three days to get everything in place if I was going to make use of the caps. My sister spent an afternoon making phone calls. After a few calls, we discovered there was one facility only in the Twin Cities metro area with a Penguin Cold Cap freezer and an oncologist familiar with the therapy. I needed an appointment with Dr. Zander at Minnesota Oncology, and I needed it within the next three days. This not only meant finding one opening, but also before I could even meet with the doctor, the clinic had to be able to schedule all eight of my chemotherapy sessions. The gentleman in scheduling chuckled when I asked if I could see Dr. Zander within the next three days, but he agreed to try. I prayed while I was on hold and when he came back on the phone, he said, "You are one lucky young lady. He had a cancellation; you can see him in two days." I knew in my heart that God was behind the scenes making arrangements for me to get this appointment. When He does little things to bless me, I call them 'God hugs.'

Even though it was short notice, I was scheduled at the hospital the next day for minor surgery; I needed a port—a small device inserted under the skin that is a quicker and less painful way to hook up an IV, instead of inserting one in your arm or hand every time you go for treatment. You are given Lidocaine to numb the area and the needle goes 'pain free' into your port. It was an extremely weird feeling to have this small device under my skin. I was somewhat soft sided, so I had room on my body to wiggle around the device a bit if you pushed it. One thing I missed terribly after surgery, and now having my port placed, was sleeping on my stomach. I'd been a tummy sleeper for years and after surgery I was no longer able to sleep in that position. It took a few months to get accustomed to sleeping on my side.

Day one of chemotherapy doubled as cold-cap-training day. In order for the caps to work successfully, a minimum of two people are required to assist during every treatment, anyone who would possibly be coming to chemo with me had to come in for the training. One nice thing about using the cold caps is you get a private room for your treatment because of the freezer's location where the caps are kept. We got our own room with a large TV, which we never turned on, a couple of chairs, and little bit of room for the nurses and those coming with to help me. Everyone in my support team learned how to use the caps that day. After seeing how involved the process is, I was thankful for the extra training everyone received. The caps contain dry ice and are semi-soft-sided helmets of sorts that are tightly strapped on your head. It's a very precise process; those helping are required to wear special gloves and must continually check the temperature of the caps, switching them out exactly every 26 minutes. If the cap isn't put on correctly or cold enough, it could then result in sections of hair loss. Essentially, the hair follicles covered by the cap freeze. As a result, the chemo drugs are prevented from causing these follicles to die, which is what causes hair loss. Needless to say, it was a lot of work! And since cold cap therapy is not covered by insurance, some very sweet family friends offered to pay for the treatments—*another God-hug.*

Had I lost all my hair, it would have been difficult, but I would have gotten over it. I was more concerned about the effect my hair loss would have on my kids. In recent years, one grandpa had died from cancer, and they had seen their other grandpa lose his hair and eventually pass away from cancer too. I was worried that if they saw me losing my hair, then it would remind them of how sick cancer made their grandpas and their eventual passing away. I didn't want them coming home from school every day, seeing me looking sick and worrying about my health. My kids were the driving force behind most of the decisions I made regarding my breast cancer treatments, cold cap therapy included.

The morning of my first treatment I was in good spirits, laughing with my mom and sister on our way to the clinic. We had to be on the road early because of rush hour traffic. I jumped into the car with a cup of coffee and my bag that included my pillow, my daughter's homemade fleece tie blanket, magazines, snacks, and movies. In my Instagram post that morning, coffee in hand, I smiled for the camera. I believe my post read something like, "Headed to my first chemo today. After today only seven more to go!" *I was clueless to what I was in for.*

The cold cap treatments required a two-hour head start and two hours post treatment. The actual treatment time was two hours, making it all a long six-hour process. My eight scheduled treatments were divided into 4 sessions, each with different types of chemotherapy meds. The first was what is commonly referred to as 'the red devil' because the medication is actually red, and it is the one med that typically causes nausea and hair loss. After labs and a short visit with Dr. Zander, we made ourselves at home in our room. The Penguin cold cap representative was there and ready to start. We started the first cap at 7:30 am. I tried to be positive and laugh as we used panty liners around the edges of my face to avoid freezer burn. The laughing was short lived—the caps were colder than I could have imagined. They gave me the most painful brain freeze headache you can imagine. I've never had a migraine, but from how others have described them to me, this headache must have been similar. As soon as the intense pain from the cold cap started to wear off, it was be time to switch caps again. Every 26 minutes was another wave of pain.

We started the chemotherapy medication two hours after the cold cap treatments began. I still hadn't adjusted to using the caps as I sat in my reclining chair with a blanket, my pillow, and slippers. I was ready to start the first phase of my treatment. The nurse administering the meds was kind and caring. You could tell she had administered these same drugs to probably thousands of other women. She knew just what to say to keep me as calm as possible. She suggested I eat a popsicle to help prevent sores from developing in my mouth. I looked at her like she was crazy as I sat there with dry ice on my head. But I did it; I didn't want to deal with mouth sores on top of everything else. It wasn't ten minutes into receiving the drugs that I began to sob uncontrollably. I can't explain it. I don't remember anything that particularly bothered me, yet I basically lost it. I could not get myself under control. The nurse sitting next to me explained it was normal and that my 'chemo cocktail' also included meds for anxiety. I was so confused until my main nurse, Jane—who, by the way, I adore—came over and patted me on the arm gently. "It's okay. This is totally normal. You are just having an anxiety attack." I looked right up at her and replied, "I don't have those." The truth was, she was right. I felt panicked. I felt out of control. I felt out of sorts. I felt sick. It was all awful. I cried almost the entire six hours I was there, and to this day, I can't explain why, other than it was exactly what my nurse said it was, anxiety.

> It wasn't ten minutes into receiving the drugs that I began to sob uncontrollably. I can't explain it. I don't remember anything that particularly bothered me, yet I basically lost it. I could not get myself under control. The nurse sitting next to me explained it was normal and that my 'chemo cocktail' also included meds for anxiety.

That first treatment felt like it lasted forever. I felt panicky on the inside the entire day, not wanting anyone to leave my side for even a moment. Even though I knew intellectually that everything was going to be okay, I couldn't get my mind to be quiet or my emotions under control. I suppose I didn't really need to, but I didn't like how out of control I was feeling. My mom and sister stayed with me the entire day while the others who came to help went home. We never turned on the TV or any music. I never ate a thing; I just tried to drink the water I was asked to drink. All I could think about was counting down how many more cold caps I needed to endure before my time was up. Kelsey figured out how many we'd have to switch out based on the 26-minute switch time, so she'd write the number on a white board, and we would cross them off as we went along. Jeff came down that afternoon to pick me up and bring me home. My head hurt so incredibly bad that I tried not to open my eyes any more than necessary. I wrapped myself up in my blanket because I had literally been on dry ice all day. I was freezing, even though it was June and in the 90's outside. I hadn't eaten that day, so on the way home, I wanted something in my stomach. The problem was nothing sounded even remotely good. I settled on a vanilla shake from McDonalds, which I didn't finish.

My second treatment went much better, maybe it was because I knew what to expect, or I possibly didn't feel quite so out of control. Either way, it was a better day. The cold caps were still terribly painful, and I just sat in my chair with my blanket, closing my eyes in between caps changing, trying to rest. Kelsey took charge of the caps, keeping the timing on track and making sure each person that came to help knew exactly what to do. She also had the job of taking me to the bathroom. Sisters are the best. We had to carefully time bathroom breaks because we had the 26-minute time frame for switching out caps to adhere to. It felt like *so much work* to use the restroom—we had to get slippers on me, wrap me up in a blanket, unplug my IV and untangle the cords, and then help me walk to the bathroom that was just outside our room. She had to hold the IV cords out of the way for me, not to mention adhering to the 'rules' for using the toilet while under chemo. I often wonder what the other patients, also having treatment, thought when they heard us laughing in the bathroom. I decided early on that I'd rather laugh about the situation and how ridiculous the entire thing was because the alternative was to cry. The people who came to the cold cap training and my first treatment rotated treatments so that the same

I looked on and noticed something unexpected; he was wearing pink cleats and pink gloves—*in my honor!* That thoughtful surprise from my 18-year-old son was another God-hug. Tears ran down my cheeks not only because it was such a public sign of love for me, but also because I was so proud of what an amazing young man he'd become.

people didn't have to come every single time; except my mom and sister who were there every single time. One of my best friends, Jerra, even tried a cold cap on her head during one of my treatments just to get an idea of what I was going through. It was one of the kindest gestures of friendship I've experienced; it was a God-hug.

The first four treatments left me feeling nauseous for days. I honestly lived on Sally's Pita Chips because it was the only thing that sat well in my stomach. I was on an every-other-week schedule. And just about the time the nausea started to wear off, I'd have to go back and start the process again. Treatments five through eight included a new set of chemo medications, of course, with different side effects. After the last treatments, I had terrible body aches, even my bones hurt. It was hard to sleep in the days following these treatments because even the slightest touch from anyone was painful. I was now also being sent to a clinic closer to my house the day after each treatment because it became a two-day process. I had to have a shot and a four-hour IV to help me stay hydrated. Those days were difficult. I was in so much pain, and the recliners at the clinic were incredibly uncomfortable. My aunt Teppe and my mom took turns driving me and sitting with me at my day-two appointments; I hated those days too.

I truly believe something positive can be found in even the most negative situations. While I have many personal examples to share from my time with breast cancer alone, I'll share one that was particularly significant to me. I had my eighth chemotherapy treatment scheduled so I would be finished before my son's football season started in early September. It was his senior year, and I refused to miss a single one of his eight regular-season games. I had my last session on a Tuesday and attended his first game of the season that Friday night. I didn't feel great, but I was there. As I sat in the stands, returning to my alma mater, I cheered for the black and orange Osseo Senior High Varsity football team. As they ran onto the field, I watched closely for #4. The starting defensive line came onto the field, getting into position for the first play of the game when I spotted him. I looked on and noticed something unexpected; he was wearing pink cleats and pink gloves—*in my honor!* That thoughtful surprise from my 18-year-old son was another God-hug. Tears ran down my cheeks not only because it was such a public sign of love for me, but also because I was so proud of what an amazing young man he'd become. I watched him in play after play, tackle after tackle, helping his team win the game, and his pink cleats became the way I could always spot him on the field. I wanted to yell to everyone in our section, "Hey, that's my kid with the sack! He's the one wearing pink cleats *for me!*"

After wrapping up my eighth treatment sessions, I had another important decision to make. This time it was whether I would or would not have radiation treatment. The first radiologist told me I was in the gray area, whatever that means, basically telling me I could go either way. I was so frustrated when I left the appointment that I was in tears. All I could think was *You're the doctor; you tell me!* We made an appointment with a second radiologist who gave me a more solid answer. He told me he was okay with me choosing not to have radiation; however, if I had it, then I could reduce my chance of recurrence by another 7 to 10%. After what my kids had been through with both parents, I was determined to do everything possible to make sure they'd never have to worry about me again. I asked my radiologist to schedule me for the daily treatments.

Before starting the 28-day cycle, I had to have a form cast of my body to make sure I lined up correctly every single time I lied down for treatment. The radiation machine had to be precise in order to hit the exact same spots each day of treatment. They drew four black-dot tattoos on me, which were used to line up the radiation machine each day in the exact spot needed. The technicians whom I saw every day were great; they became like friends by the end of the process.

It seemed like I had a knack for awkward moments while I battled cancer, and radiation was no different. Each day, when I was getting into position on the radiation table, the machine above me was lined up perfectly with my tiny tattoos. We did, however, have one issue when getting me into position every day. My right breast was a little too big and, thus, in the way of one of the lines of radiation. In order to get the straight shot to one particular spot on my left side, the male technician needed to tape my breast down and out of the way. He did this every single day. One morning, while lying on the radiation table with no top on, I patiently waited for the five technicians and nurses to get me into the correct position. The male technician ripped off tape from its roll, and while pushing my breast out of the way, he made small talk by saying, "I know a guy from your church." I thought to myself *Did he really just say that? At the exact moment he is taping my breast?* I could not wait to get in the car and call my sister to laugh about it.

The radiation was tiring. I had to be at the clinic by 9 am every morning for nearly a month straight, not to mention having to deal with the snow during a Minnesota winter. The effects of radiation, for most people, are cumulative. This means that as the days progress, the side effect grow worse. The radiation started to really wear on me by day 14 of 28. Even though my radiologist had prescribed cream to protect my skin, the treatments started to burn. Once that burning process started, the burn area grew larger every day. My skin was red and irritated, and if I didn't hold my arm in a certain way, the burn would crack even more. I was so incredibly thankful to finish my last day of treatment the week before Christmas. I needed the rest before the holiday. The next couple of months were a time for me to catch up on rest and allow my body to truly heal from the trauma of the past eight months.

> I had faced dark times, overcome loss, and dealt with disappointment—but cancer was different. I had to be resilient for my kids because I wanted them to see me being strong and brave, and not just hear me talk about it.

Fighting cancer gave me an entirely new perspective on grit. I had faced dark times, overcome loss, and dealt with disappointment—but cancer was different. I had to be resilient for my kids because I wanted them to see me being strong and brave, and not just hear me talk about it. One of my goals throughout the entire process was for my children to see me pushing back against cancer, fighting for me and for them. At the same time, it was important for me to be authentic, allowing them to see my tears and pain, never wanting to give a false impression that everything was perfect. I wanted them to see a realistic picture of cancer while changing the narrative of loss they had experienced with both of their grandpas—*and I did.*

A Grit Girl is <u>DESTINED</u> to be <u>INSPIRING</u>.

I found several positives in my breast cancer. The largest by far has been the ability to inspire other women. Your story is no different; you were destined to have a story to tell and when you fight through your darkest times, you become an inspiration. You are destined to inspire. *You are a Grit Girl.*

"I will give thanks and praise to the LORD, with all my heart;

I will tell aloud all Your wonders and marvelous deeds."

Psalm 9:1 The Amplified Bible

CHAPTER 10

DEPRESSION, DISHES & DREAMS

IN APRIL 2013 I WAS SCHEDULED FOR CT SCANS PRIOR TO MY ONE-YEAR follow-up appointment with my oncologist. I had mixed emotions leading up to the day of what would be a significant appointment in my recovery process. This visit was the one we'd been waiting for, the one letting us know whether the cancer was completely gone, *or if it wasn't.* In my heart of hearts, I knew I was cancer free and aside from the final reconstructive surgery, my physical battle was over. But I still had lingering fear and continual 'what if' thoughts. What helped me suppress some of these scary thoughts was my confidence in every step taken by my doctors to make me cancer-free and, more so, my trust in Jesus. I had one goal in mind, one sentence I wanted to hear, one statement I wanted to report, and it revolved around two words: cancer free. I didn't sleep well the night before my appointment, my emotions ranging from excited to hear the good news to anxious that something else could show up in either the scans or the labs. Four people were in the forefront of my mind, the ones most important to me who needed to hear these words the most: Carter, Brock, Tucker, and Kennedy.

I had my scans across the street from my clinic. They weren't near as suffocating a feeling as an MRI. I so badly wanted to ask the technicians what they saw, even though I knew they couldn't give me any indication of the results. As I walked back across the street to Dr. Zander's office, I could feel the sunshine on my face and smell the fresh spring air. I felt like I could burst on the inside, wanting to tell every person I walked by that I was diagnosed with breast cancer a year ago and today I was pretty sure I'd find out it was gone. It's a weird feeling to be at the hospital and clinic because your story is so personal and big to you that it's easy to forget every person you encounter in those settings has a story too.

> I could feel the sunshine on my face and smell the fresh spring air. I felt like I could burst on the inside, wanting to tell every person I walked by that I was diagnosed with breast cancer a year ago and today I was pretty sure I'd find out it was gone.

After checking in and talking with nurse Jane (my favorite), Jeff and I were alone for a few moments while we waited for Dr. Zander to come in. My eyes swelled up with tears looking at Jeff. I said, "Can you even believe what we just went through this past year? On some level, I was still incredulous at the idea that I had battled breast cancer and had multiple surgeries, chemotherapy, and radiation. Sometimes, it even felt like it was someone else's story not mine. Doc was quick to get to the details, of course, knowing were on pins and needles to hear what he had to say. He was happy to report that he was going to classify me as 'in remission.' In my terms, I called that *cancer free*. Jeff and I looked at each other, both of us relieved. My immediate thought was that I couldn't wait to tell the kids. I wanted any fear about my health erased from their thinking. The appointment was good news. Dr. Zander was happy with the scans and labs and happy but somewhat guarded about the future; he was optimistic. I believe at the time of that appointment, he felt there was only a 13% chance of re-occurrence; in my mind there as 0%. We discussed a follow-up plan, which included genetic counseling, appointments every three months for a year, and Tamoxifen, the medication I would need to take for the next ten years.

I thought I'd be happier than I actually was after hearing those two words. I'd been dealing with anxiety, even some depression on a small scale, which I had contributed to not knowing whether the cancer was gone or not. While I was overjoyed to call myself a breast cancer survivor, I still felt anxious, not at all back to being *myself*. I felt lost as if underwater trying to reach the surface of 'normal.' No matter how hard I kicked to reach the top, it was still out of reach. The anxiety I experienced during my first chemo treatment stayed with me. It was not like me to ignore the things around me that needed to be done. *But I just didn't care.*

I was also easily frazzled by the thought of going anywhere. To run a simple errand felt overwhelming, and my poor kids regularly asked where all the food because I didn't feel up to grocery shopping. I really didn't want to leave my house; I wanted to hide. I had this idea that I'd at least lose weight after going through breast cancer, especially chemotherapy—*but no, I gained weight.* In general, I didn't feel great. And on top of it, I didn't feel good about how I looked. The thought of going to an event made me feel sick. This was another indicator that I wasn't myself. I'm normally the first of my friends to suggest a night out. An extrovert by nature, I'm not one to turn down a good time. During the two years after my diagnosis, I was tired, irritable, and not social. In fact, I found out later that one of my good friends at the time had complained about including me for 'girl time,' going so far as to say she wished I would 'snap out of it.' She expressed her feelings that I wasn't fun to hang out with anymore. Even my friends noticed that I wasn't me. My true friends didn't complain; they loved me through it all.

My entire life I was a person who couldn't sit still. For years, after the kids were in bed, I'd walk around the house picking up toys, washing dishes, and folding laundry. Jeff would say to me all the time, "Can't you ever just sit down and relax?" My response was always the same, "I can't relax looking at a mess or knowing there are dirty dishes in the sink." We would laugh if he got up for any reason in the morning because I'd make the bed before he returned. He'd often find it neatly put together. "Can't you leave the bed unmade for more than 10 minutes?" he'd ask every single time. I would just shake my head, "No, no I cannot." I hated seeing a messy bed, and I'd also make all the kids' beds every morning. Cancer cured me of that; now I can count on one hand the few times I make my bed in an entire month. I was the mom who couldn't sleep if the dirty dishes weren't loaded, the one who challenged herself daily to have *all* the laundry done, folded, and put away. I spent more time than I'd like to think about vacuuming and picking up after the four kids. In fact, I spent too much time cleaning. Period. My mentality took an enormous out-of-balance shift. Before cancer, I was too worried about the house being picked up. After cancer, I just didn't care.

After talking to my nurse at one of my follow-up appointments about how I was feeling, she explained that anxiety was one of the side effects of Tamoxifen, the medication I was required to take post breast cancer. She even said, "The meds will make you feel 'que sara sara'—like you just don't care." She was right. That was exactly how I felt. Over the year and a half of regular appointments with my oncologist, I mentioned several times that I was feeling anxious. Each time he encouraged me to give myself time to adjust to the medication. It really bothered me that I didn't feel like cooking, cleaning or doing laundry—all things a mother of four should be doing consistently. I didn't attend church regularly or even the kids' games. These were clear signs that I was wasn't myself. My mom gave me an old blue recliner that was extremely comfortable. And even though it looked like an old-dad chair, I put it in our main living room. I ended up sitting in it and, sometimes, even sleeping in it for the better part of two years. Looking back, I may have been suffering from mild depression. The anxious and somewhat depressed person I was at the time was radically different from who I'd been my whole life and even who I am today.

Many things made me feel anxious or sad, but they were often unpredictable. One of those moments that particularly bothered me was completely unexpected. On the way home from one of my chemotherapy treatments, I noticed a woman running along the side of the road. I started crying because all I could think was *I can't do that. Even if I wanted to run, I simply can't.* Prior to cancer, I was accustomed to working out a minimum of five days a week and had done so consistently for 15 years. I knew I didn't feel physically up to working out, but seeing someone running on the same path where I used to run really bothered me. The thought of not having the ability to do something I really wanted to do was depressing. I would have given anything to have the strength and the desire to get out and run. Even now after five years, I've had a difficult time getting back into a consistent work-out routine.

I can't explain the exact moment that my anxiety and depression were gone. I suppose part of it was just a matter of time, and like my nurse Jane had said, adjusting to medications. The bigger part, though, was something much bigger than me. Throughout this process, I tried my best to put my trust in Jesus and depend on His grace to get me through. I'll be honest; I didn't always do a great job of it, but I never got the feeling He minded. He was always there. Pushing through wasn't just about me, it was about the driving forces behind my fight. My will to beat cancer, survive for my family, and my dependence on Jesus' grace are what enabled me to do it. Showing my kids what it meant not to give up in the face of a ginormous obstacle was important to me. However, I believe that not having kids wouldn't have changed my approach or decision making much; it just made it feel all the more important. I tapped into something that gave me the strength to fight not only cancer, but also the after effects. Many days I didn't feel strong. I didn't feel like engaging in day-to-day life, but eventually I had to decide I didn't care how I felt. I was going to do it anyway.

> My will to beat cancer, survive for my family, and my dependence on Jesus' grace are what enabled me to do it. Showing my kids what it meant not to give up in the face of a ginormous obstacle was important to me.

I actually believe two factors brought me out of my anxiety and depression. The first was talking to other women facing breast cancer or other significant setbacks. It was tremendously helpful for me to reach out to others. In fact, it was more than helpful; it was healing. The more I took the focus off myself and what I was dealing with, the more I was able to put it in the past. When you sit with your problem for an extended period of time, it can become easy to forget that others around you are in pain too. Choosing to focus on other people gets your eyes off self. Whenever I found the opportunity to talk to someone who needed a pick me up, I'd take it. Women who had been recently diagnosed would call me, and I enjoyed taking time to talk to them. Every conversation I had with other women facing cancer reminded me of the one-hour talk I had with the pastor who called me, so when I was able to do the same for someone else, it fed my soul.

The second factor that helped me push through the residual anxiety was the result of a conversation with my oldest son, Carter. One day while watching Survivor, our favorite TV show, he casually said, "Mom, you beat cancer. You can do anything! I think you should go for your dream." The dream took courage to follow and almost as much grit to fight cancer. In fact, I had to be physically, emotionally, and spiritually tough to embrace my dream—and do you know what? *I was.* Together, Carter and I applied to be on the Emmy award winning reality TV series. I received a call back, but it didn't go any further than the initial call. Once Carter convinced me to submit my application, there was no stopping me. The next fall I applied a second time, received another call back, and was invited to participate in the interview process. In March of 2016, I received a call that changed my life, again. I was invited to participate in the 33rd season of the show that I loved and the game I had dreamed about playing for years. Later that fall, I held viewing parties and sat in my living room in awe of the fact that I was now watching myself compete in Survivor Millennials vs Gen-X—my dream come true. The more important thing is knowing that even though I had experienced a

> Together, Carter and I applied to be on the Emmy award winning reality TV series. I received a call back, but it didn't go any further than the initial call. Once Carter convinced me to submit my application, there was no stopping me.

difficult few years, I truly believe something positive can come out of any negative situation, and I'm confident that the doors opened by my participation on Survivor are a result of having the title Breast Cancer Survivor. I'm not sure I would have dug deep enough to find the strength, the bravery and, most importantly, the grit to tackle something like Survivor. I was not only a survivor in more ways than one, but also I was able to accomplish both because of grit.

A Grit Girl is <u>DESIGNED</u> to be <u>TOUGH</u>.

As women, while we are all unique, having differing personalities and talents, one thing we all share is the fortitude to be physically and emotionally tough— when we need to be. Women possess the unique ability to float between soft and tough, depending on what is needed in the moment and with whom. Girl, when the tough get going, so do you because you were designed tough. *You are a Grit Girl.*

"She is clothed with strength and dignity and she laughs without fear at the future."

Proverbs 31:25 The Message Translation

CHAPTER 11
MDS, MOM & MOTIVATION

TWO YEARS AFTER MY DIAGNOSIS, I STILL DIDN'T FEEL TOTALLY BACK TO myself, so adding another difficult situation was especially over-whelming. In September 2013, I found myself in another doctor's office awaiting tests—this time for my mom. Having to meet with a doctor at the University of Minnesota should have been the first indicator it would most likely not be good news. The room started to spin and her doctor, Dr. Cooley, began to explain Myelodysplastic syndrome (MDS), an auto-immune disease and a form of cancer of the blood. A few minutes into

> In September 2013, I found myself in another doctor's office awaiting tests—this time for my mom.

her explanation she started to sound like Charlie Brown's teacher. Trying to break it down into layman's terms, she used the word leukemia. In essence, MDS was a time bomb inside of her body; at any moment her cells could morph from MDS to leukemia. *I wanted to punch the wall.* The conversation ended with a recommendation for a bone marrow transplant and a statement I'll never forget: "If the cells develop into leukemia, I give her eight weeks to live." Dr. Cooley said this in the most delicate way she could.

We were stunned. My mom, my Aunt Teppe and me just sat there. I walked out of the room, not wanting my mom to see how upset I was. One by one, I called my siblings. Whenever I have important information, I have a system, starting with my oldest brother down to my sister. My brothers are much calmer than I am. They simply responded with an "okay." This made three years in a row of major medical situations, starting with Jeff in 2011, my breast cancer in 2012, and now my mom's diagnosis in 2013. How could this be happening again? Cancer again? More appointments, doctors, and hospitals. I felt like I hadn't fully dealt with what I'd just been through, let alone have to deal with worrying about my mom too. I knew I'd need to be strong for her in the coming months. As the oldest, I felt completely responsible for her care; I was her advocate. Once again, I tried my best to be strong. *I needed to be a Grit Girl for her.*

> This made three years in a row of major medical situations, starting with Jeff in 2011, my breast cancer in 2012, and now my mom's diagnosis in 2013. How could this be happening again? Cancer again?

My mom wasn't ready for a bone marrow transplant as soon as her doctors would have liked and definitely not as soon as I would have liked. I couldn't make her schedule it—as much as I wanted. She had a little sister, Leslie, who she watched pass away from leukemia when Leslie was only five years old. My mom took her to chemotherapy treatments, so she saw how the medications, especially the prednisone, affected Leslie. My mom wanted nothing to do with it.

In January 2015, my mom scheduled the bone marrow transplant. Her doctor told us that once in the hospital she would be getting a massive dose of chemotherapy that would cause her hair to fall out. Instead of worrying about it in the hospital, Kelsey and I spent the evening at my mom's while my aunt cut off her beautiful hair completely. We have a picture of her head being shaved and in the background, you can see me with my head in my hands crying. My mom loves her hair; we often tease her that she should have been born in Texas because she loves Texas-sized hair. She handled it like the strong woman she always is. We went to the bathroom together, cried together, and then laughed together—convincing ourselves it would all be okay. I tried to be strong for my mom. On top of what she was already dealing with, I didn't want her worried about me too.

My mom's favorite time of year is Christmas, and we did our best to make it as nice as possible, knowing she was going to check in to the hospital on January 5. A typical bone marrow transplant patient is in the hospital for up to 30 days. My mom likes to be busy, so sitting in the hospital for a month sounded awful to her, as I'm sure it would to anyone. After being admitted, one of her first questions was to her designated nurse: "What is the fastest time anyone has been discharged from here after a transplant?" The nurse replied, "I believe one gentleman was out in 13 days, but that is highly unusual." My mom decided she was going to beat the record and go home quicker than anyone else at the U of M. Her room was regulated for pure air, had alarms on the door, and special rules to enter. I had to keep a separate set of clothes to wear and a blanket to use in her room. I spent the night with her the first few nights, just like she'd done for me when I had surgery. On day three she had chemotherapy and a high dose of radiation. The side effects made her shake uncontrollably. I laid by her on her bed, trying to hold her body still. I played peaceful worship music to keep the room's atmosphere calm for her. The only thing worse than you feeling sick is watching someone you love go through something so difficult.

Even in the hospital, a place where most people would lay in bed and rest, my mom refused. She woke up early every morning, got dressed, put on make-up, and made her bed—every single day. Every doctor and nurse that came in was in shock that she was sitting up in bed looking like she was heading out for the day. There's nothing typical about my mom; she's tough as nails and refused to allow circumstances to dictate her life. Much to the surprise of her team of caretakers, she met every expectation given and was discharged on day ten—beating the previous record by four days. Everyone else was surprised; *I was not.*

Even though she was discharged from the hospital, she was required to have someone with her 24/7 to monitor her temperature. Her BMT doctor explained she could go from perfectly fine to a fever, and even possible death, within 20 minutes. My four siblings and I took turns sleeping overnight at her house for almost three months. We had a cot set up in the bedroom to sleep on, just in case something happened in the middle of the night. I remember driving to her house at 9pm many nights. It was during one of those weeks that she got us hooked watching the TV show Parenthood with her. Although the interruption in our lives was significant, it did give my siblings and I the opportunity to spend quality time with her individually.

Even though she was discharged from the hospital, she was required to have someone with her 24/7 to monitor her temperature. Her BMT doctor explained she could go from perfectly fine to a fever, and even possible death, within 20 minutes. My four siblings and I took turns sleeping overnight at her house for almost three months.

During those three months, I felt like my life was on hold. One night specifically, I remember having to drive to her house in the middle of a snow storm. I didn't have an option. I white-knuckled the 15-mile drive; the snow was falling so hard I couldn't see the lanes on the freeway. What would typically be a 20-minute drive took over an hour. By the time I got to her house, I cried. I had been so afraid while driving. I had to be available during the week to take her to multiple appointments, all at the University of Minnesota—a 45-minute drive one way and in the middle of winter. It wasn't her fault, but I felt like I had no life of my own. At the time I didn't allow it to bother me. I would do anything to keep my mom safe and alive. The threat that she could get sick and die was always in the back of my mind. My mom's a praying woman, and there was zero question in her mind that her trust in Jesus would see her through.

Over the next two years, my mom dealt with Graft vs Host disease, which is common after a bone marrow transplant. The disease is difficult for doctors to pin-point because it manifests itself differently in each patient. Because of the transplant, my mom's immune system was compromised, making it easier for her to get extremely sick, even from something as minor as the common cold. My mom was hospitalized several times with pneumonia and other symptoms as a direct result of the Graft vs. Host. She had regular painful bone marrow biopsies, which caused her anxiety. The anticipation of them were almost worse than the procedures themselves. Each time, I tried to calm her nerves and talk her through the appointments. One time I recorded her on her phone. I had her tell me she was fine and had her say into her phone's camera that "This is never as bad as I think it's going to be. I'm okay." I kept the recording for the next biopsy and when she started to feel worried, I played it for her to remind her, with her own words, that she didn't have anything to worry about. It worked.

Those two years felt like they were never going to end. We felt helpless while she had to suffer one setback after another. There was nothing we could do. At one point the Graft vs Host manifested on her skin. As a result, she was required to take Prednisone for six months. The steroids had awful side effects, the worst being the softening of her bones. As a result, she lost bone density, which complicated a prior osteoporosis diagnosis. One morning she stood up in bed and was immediately in incredible pain. She called me in tears, hardly able to move. I can't remember the reason, but I wasn't able to take her to emergency that morning; her roommate took her. Even though she could hardly walk, they sent her home with pain medication, telling her she probably sprained

Over the next two years, my mom dealt with Graft vs Host disease, which is common after a bone marrow transplant. The disease is difficult for doctors to pin-point because it manifests itself differently in each patient. Because of the transplant, my mom's immune system was compromised, making it easier for her to get extremely sick, even from something as minor as the common cold.

something. The next morning, I received another call from her in tears. She doesn't cry unless she's in a lot of pain. Again, she went in and again was sent home. On the third morning, I was able to take her. I called the U of M and told them we would be there when they opened, regardless if they had an opening or not. I have to insert here that her care team was amazing. Some of the issues revolved around weekend providers who were filling in. On day three she's in so much pain she could hardly talk. Once in the medical office, I demanded pain medication and told the nurse we weren't going anywhere until they figured out why she was in pain and did something about it. I was so angry that they had allowed her to be in pain and that it took three appointments to finally have someone figure out what was wrong. I believe every person dealing with a medical condition, especially life-threatening, needs an advocate in and out of the hospital. They gave her the strongest pain medication possible and sent us to get an MRI. The scans showed eight fractures in her back. After hearing the results, I was furious. My mom, trying to be tough, wouldn't complain because she always thought that maybe she was overreacting. She was definitely not overreacting, and I made sure her care team knew it. Throughout the entire process, her height went from 5'4" to 4'10". The only good news was I could now tease her about being shorter than me; she loves it when I do that.

> On day three she's in so much pain she could hardly talk. Once in the medical office, I demanded pain medication and told the nurse we weren't going anywhere until they figured out why she was in pain and did something about it. I was so angry that they had allowed her to be in pain and that it took three appointments to finally have someone figure out what was wrong.

Over the next two years, she was in and out of the hospital, had multiple surgeries, and yet every time she was in contact with her nurses and doctors, she would be laughing and friendly. Because she was so positive, even during her worst times, the staff loved talking to her. She talked about Jesus in a non-threatening way, giving away books, gifts, and treats to those who were helpful to her. This negative situation put her into a position to meet a number of people she would have never met otherwise, and she had a positive impact on every single one of them. Her positive outlook and joy were an inspiration to everyone. The appointments and setbacks eventually slowed down. Finally in 2017, she graduated from seeing her bone marrow doctor. I had to tap into grit to help carry mom through. It was ironic that the one who taught me grit and stood by my side was now the one who needed me for the same. There were late night calls, days of frustration, and times she had to be hospitalized. Through it all, I had to be the strong one. My mom is the embodiment of grit and resilience, refusing to give up and definitely designed tough. *She is a grit girl.*

A Grit Girl is <u>DESIGNED</u> to be <u>TOUGH</u>.

Negative situations can reveal something surprising: strength. It isn't until we are pushed to our limit that out of necessity we discover our true grit. Every woman is equipped with God-given strength that will carry her through her hardest times. You were designed tough; it's in your nature. Have you ever heard the term "Mama Bear"? *You are tough. You are a Grit Girl.*

"The LORD is my strength and shield. I trust him with all my heart. He helps me, and my heart is filled with joy. I burst out in songs of thanksgiving."

Psalm 28:7 The New Living Translation

CHAPTER 12

MOUNTAIN GRIT

"GO AHEAD, I'LL CATCH UP," I COULD HARDLY GET THE WORDS OUT WHILE gasping for air. We were on a family vacation in 2017, five years after the diagnosis, and I had to remind myself this was *my* idea. As we hiked up Booth Falls Trail outside Veil Colorado I thought I was literally going to keel over. Groups of wilderness experts—by experts I mean families who apparently could breathe just fine in the altitude, who had Camelback water bottles, hiking boots, and big dogs—passed us. Technically, they were passing me because the rest of my family, wearing old tennis shoes, sandals and carrying non-eco-friendly disposable water bottles, had to stop and wait for me. I was embarrassed because I hate feeling like the weak one; I didn't want to be the mom who couldn't keep up.

Brock stopped and waited for me, a typical second-born child, helpful and kind—a God-hug moment for me. I especially appreciated that he didn't seem annoyed having to wait for me, even though the hike seemed like just a walk for him. My husband was far enough ahead that he was just out of eyesight before realizing I had stopped to catch my breath on a large boulder. He quickly came back to wait with me and hang on to my arm as I tried to keep my footing on some of the steeper rocky spots. One of the things that attracted me to him 25 years earlier was the fact that he's a gentleman, always ready to help me, and anyone else; it didn't hurt his chances that he was strong too. Between breaths I tried to tell my four athletic kids and daughter-in-law they could just keep going, but they'd still periodically stop and wait; they get that from their dad. On the inside, I was telling my body to get it together and suck it up. Funny thing was I could hardly breathe, so it was particularly hard to suck anything up. I took a moment to stop on a section of trail going right through a small field full of white flowers and was overwhelmed by how beautiful it was and how fresh the air smelled.

> One of the things that attracted me to him 25 years earlier was the fact that he's a gentleman, always ready to help me, and anyone else; it didn't hurt his chances that he was strong too.

I'm not a quitter and as I looked up the trail and saw how far I still had to go, I was irritated that I wasn't in better shape. The ironic thing was I was the one who planned the hiking in the first place. And even though they were complaining about it ahead of time, they ended up loving it. *I knew I was right; I knew they'd like it.* I had to deliberately change my thoughts from "I can't do this" to "Buck up, buttercup, and just keep moving. One step at a time, you'll eventually get to the top." I decided *I'm taking this mountain; this mountain is not taking me.* I reminded myself I didn't need to conquer the mountain in one giant leap. All I had to do was dig deep and keep going. Because I couldn't see the top of the trail in the woods, I decided to focus on the smaller section right in front of me. It reminded me of Dorothy on the yellow brick road to Oz, except she had beautiful red pumps, and I was wearing old smelly running shoes.

As I kept moving, my lungs and body started to adjust. And even though the trail became steeper as we went, it actually became easier at the same time. After an hour and a half, we made it to the top of the three-mile trail, stopping along with other families right along-side a natural plateau at the waterfall. I was amazed at God's creation, beautiful beyond words. Jeff and the kids went even farther, climbing rocks and trees across the fast moving ice-cold water. I was content in my achievement of making it to the top of the trail, so I found a spot and waited as they explored the area, not feeling the need to go crazy by hanging out in frigid waters.

It was grit pushing me to keep moving, even when my chest was burning. And it was grit that prevented me from giving up when facing hardship. Troubling times provide the opportunity to discover strength and reveal grit. My life has been a lot like this hiking trail in Colorado—at times I've to stop and catch my breath; other times I had to dig deep, forcing myself to keep moving. I had to tap into my grit.

I didn't realize it then, but the storms I've faced have been times of transformation, reminding me of the necklace I'd been given with the words: NO GRIT NO PEARL.

The list of negatives my family and I have experienced during the last 20 years feels long, yet some I haven't gone into detail about because they are not my story to tell. As a family, we've faced loss, not only our grandpas and our life-threatening medical crises, but heroin addiction, miscarriages, a stillborn nephew, and another nephew born as a micro-preemie. Even though each situation required inner strength, it was a process to find it, and it happened differently for every person involved. On the other side of these life altering storms that we all faced, if we looked back, I think we'd realize we are much more alike than we are different. I hope as you read the stories I shared from my heart, you were able to picture yourself and possibly the storm you are facing right now. I'm not special, more versed in

> As a family, we've faced loss, not only our grandpas and our life-threatening medical crises, but heroin addiction, miscarriages, a stillborn nephew, and another nephew born as a micro-preemie. Even though each situation required inner strength, it was a process to find it, and it happened differently for every person involved.

the Bible, or more qualified than the next gal. I simply believe we've all been given an inner strength that sometimes we don't realize is there until we need it. I truly hope I've accomplished my goal of convincing you that you already possess the inner strength to make it through anything. You are dependent on grace, defined by resilience, destined to be an inspiration, and you are one tough cookie. *You've got grit; you are a Grit Girl!*

The foundation of my story includes my trust in Jesus. He was the constant that made me strong, and it was His grace that gave me ability do what I could not do on my own. He provided the inner strength I needed—it was grit. He's responsible for the transformation in me, taking grit and making it beautiful. He's waiting to do the same for you!

A PRAYER FOR YOU

"Heavenly Father,

I pray for the woman reading this book, the one facing her own mountain.

I pray you demonstrate your love to her in a tangible way.

I ask you Father to give her the strength she needs to keep going and never give up.

I thank you that you've already made her a Grit Girl and that you are teaching her how to find herself.

In Jesus Name, Amen."

A SCRIPTURE FOR YOU

"Trust in and rely confidently on the LORD with all your heart

And do not rely on your own insight or understanding.

In all your ways know and acknowledge and recognize Him,

And He will make your paths straight and smooth

[removing obstacles that block your way]."

Proverbs 3:5-6 The Amplified Bible

NO GRIT NO PEARL